PHILOSOPHY IN THE KITCHEN.

PHILOSOPHY

IN

THE KITCHEN:

GENERAL HINTS ON FOODS AND DRINKS.

BY

AN OLD BOHEMIAN.

ISBN 978-1-4067-9619-3

TO THE

SAVAGE CLUB.

CONTENTS.

PART IV.

POULTRY AND GAME—FISH AND SHELLFISH—MOLLUSCS AND TURTLE.

PHILOSOPHY IN THE KITCHEN.

PRELIMINARY REMARKS.

I BEG to disclaim, at the outset, all and every notion of wishing to add to the already sufficiently bewildering store of Kitchen Manuals, Cookery Guides, and miscellaneous compilations of culinary receipts collected from all parts of the globe.

Still less is this little book meant for a didactic treatise on cookery.

My aspirations soar not so high.

My humble aim and purpose, simply, is to tender a few general hints, more or less practical, on foods and drinks and their preparation, the outcome of long observation and experience in many lands and in many kitchens—high and humble.

Receipts of dishes, a little out of the common, will be found occasionally incorporated in the text. These are given mostly by way of illustration; they are intended

B

also, somewhat ambitiously, perhaps, to stand for the fruit in the humble pudding which I diffidently venture to set before the public; whilst the anecdotes and small talk interspersed here and there, will, I hope, be indulgently permitted to pass for the peel and spices.

It may be well, also, to frankly disclaim all pretensions on my part to lecture *ex cathedrâ* on the fine-art science of kitchening even within the restricted limits indicated, though I may occasionally seem to adopt the lecturing style, as the nature of the subject, indeed, requires. I am not a professed *chef*, but simply an earnest observant amateur, who thinks, maybe without sufficient reason, that he may add a hint or two to the vast store of culinary precepts. A distinguished organ of the Press declared quite recently that "if a cookery book contain but one workable recipe which was not so before, all the rest may be leather and prunelle, and yet the book worth its price." Why not hope then that a few of my hints may be found workable?

This little book is of necessity essentially fragmentary and limited in scope and extent. It can, therefore, but lightly touch upon a few branches of the vast subject of foods and drinks and their preparation, whilst leaving many others nearly altogether unnoticed.

INTRODUCTION.

MAN has been defined, not altogether infelicitously I think, though somewhat crudely, perhaps, and flippantly, as an animal that prefers a properly cooked meal to raw food, and Noah's wine to Adam's ale—to express it shortly and neatly. Taking this definition to be apposite in the main, we may surely be permitted to assume that the proper preparation of foods and drinks should be held to constitute an essential branch of the art and science of living, at least in its more material aspects and bearings; and if we are justified in this assumption, it follows naturally that our girls, at least, ought to be theoretically and practically instructed in the principles and elements of this branch in its several degrees, according to their divers stations in life. Nay, for the matter of that, I will go even farther. I believe a theoretical and practical knowledge of the proper preparation of, at least, the common articles of food and the simpler drinks, to be as essential to man as it is admittedly to woman.

Were the truth and importance of this proposition

but practically recognised—axiomatically established, as it were—many of the ills that flesh is heir to would soon have to take their departure.

As matters actually stand in this respect, however, very few of our girls even are ever taught the merest principles and rudiments of the vitally important science of the kitchen and the cellar, or of the practical art branch of it.

Not that I mean to say simple instruction in such principles and rudiments, or even the most perfect and exhaustive training in the theory and practice of cooking will of itself suffice to turn out great and good cooks. Very far from it.

What is said of the poet may be applied equally to the cook. As the one so the other is *born* not *made*. The poet and the cook alike are nature's own handiwork, not the laborious product of training and teaching. It may sound extravagant and hyperbolic, yet I hold that our grand culinary *chefs* and blue ribbons have in their inspirations and aspirations some of the divine afflatus. If we award the laurel to Tennyson we must concede the bay to Francatelli.

La Poésie du Goût would, indeed, be a fitting complement of *La Physiologie du Goût;* only where is the *Brillat-Savarin* to chant it ?

Yet the same as a great many men and women with little or no poetry in their souls can be taught the art of rhyming and versifying, and may produce tolerably good and smooth lines ; so numbers of girls, even in the humblest walks of life, may by precept and practice be raised considerably above the low level of the scullery ; and though they may not aspire to achieve the high distinction of the culinary Order of the Blue Ribbon, and rule the roast as head cooks, yet they may be successfully trained to become very excellent cookers.

And, after all, epicures requiring the select ministrations of Archimagiri form but a limited class, whilst the immense majority of the denizens of this globe of ours are always willing to put up quite contentedly with infinitely less exquisite treatment of their palates. Moreover, high gastronomy is but too often achieved at the cost of the great digester, and at the risk of more or less serious injury to health.

Now, bearing all these things duly in mind, and carefully weighing and considering them, I think it the wiser course for me also to abstain from attempting to soar in the higher regions of my theme—and for sufficient reason. " We cannot fly. Why can we not fly ? " asks the Rev. Chadband. " No wings," suggests little Snagsby, with the brevity of wit and wisdom. " The bearing of this lies in the application of it," which is pretty obvious here. I will, therefore, in this little book keep, as far as practicable, to the humbler branches of the subject.

It is by no means unlikely, I am afraid, that some of the hints given by me may be thought a trifle over trivial, or even may lay me open to sneering comments upon my presumption in professing to teach grand-mothers the simple art of sucking eggs.

I humbly plead guilty to the charge, but I would urge in extenuation my belief that there may be some granddaughters, at least, that stand in need of such rudimentary instruction, and perhaps even not a few grandmothers whose remembrance of the lessons of their earlier life may occasionally require a little reviving.

Some months ago I came accidentally upon a little book with "Don't" on the title page, if I misremember not. Among other items of sage advice there was a caution to young people *not* to use their knife to carry the food to the mouth. Well, I thought at the time the author might have omitted such an extremely common-place and apparently superfluous injunction. Since then, however, I have had occasion to see, even in generally genteel families, the knife used in lieu of the fork, and this by children of more than twelve.

PART I.

THE FOOD OF MAN.

THIS little book is not intended, of course, for a physiological or chemical essay. Still, a few general propositions and remarks, by way of introduction to this part, may not be deemed altogether out of place here.

All material life may be said to move in an everlasting round of incessant changes, from the inorganic to the organic; from the vegetable to the animal division of nature, and back again, in endless rotation through time—and eternity.

All living organic beings—animals and plants alike—have to live in a certain measure upon air and water.

The plant feeds besides upon the soil on which it grows, drawing from it all the other elements it requires for its sustenance and development.

The animal, again, feeds, in addition, on the plant directly or indirectly, incorporating, proximately or ultimately, in its own structure the elements drawn by the latter from the earth, the water, and the air.

In its turn the vegetable comes to live on the animal; on the air it breathes forth; on the secretions and waste it throws off, and finally, directly or indirectly, on the defunct animal body itself.

Earth and air again claim plant and animal alike— and so life circles on in infinite enlinkment.

All plants and all animals have assigned them, each after its kind and nature, a certain more or less limited range of foods, beyond which they may not stray. To man alone this general rule does not rigidly apply. To him Divine beneficence has been exceptionally good. He may, more or less, freely command an almost infinite number and variety of foods. Man is created omnivorous, let crotcheters and fadists gainsay as they may, and his range of foods extends over the three great divisions of nature, for even the earth numbers among its components certain minerals that rank as important constituents of man's food.

Not that the wide range of foods open to man involves by any means the necessity or even the practicability that he should as widely avail himself of all and every of them, or even simply of those that he finds placed around him or within his reach. Many and various are the causes and circumstances that exercise a powerful determining influence over the choice of the food upon which man has to subsist—as age, for instance, climate, seasons, exertion, idiosyncrasies, social position, &c., &c.

But as the function of food may, in the widest sense, be taken to be the renewal of the material consumed in the various processes of life, including, of course, the great heating process, this one fact stands clearly out, viz., that the food which man requires for his sustenance must contain, in proper proportion, all the constituent elements of the human body ; and that it is most desirable also that these elements should exist in the food in combinations more or less identical severally with the structures of the body, so that the food need not be laboriously resolved into its elements, to be re-formed into new combinations, suitable for assimilation and incorporation. It is for this reason that animal food is more easily and more readily assimilated than vegetable food, and that a larger bulk of the latter is required to provide the same given amount of nutriment as the former.

Foods may be said to be the more perfect the more of such directly assimilable combinations they contain.

The chief materials of which the various structures of the body are severally composed may be briefly enumerated as follows :—

Water — required to maintain the indispensable fluidity of the vital juices; fat—the reserve store of combustible matter, generated from saccharine and other carbonaceous substances ; fibrin, albumen, gelatin, chondrin, &c.—salts of potash, soda, lime, magnesia,

sulphur, iron and manganese; sulphuric, hydrochloric,
phosphoric, and fluoric acids, &c., &c.

The daily waste of all these has to be supplied in
the food.

It would lead us too far here to discuss the various
classifications of food.

The usual division into two principal classes is amply
sufficient for the purpose we have here in view.

These two principal classes are—(1) the so-called
flesh forming or nitrogenous foods; and (2) the heat gene-
rating or carbonaceous foods, so termed after the two chief
purposes for which food is required by the body, viz., to
generate heat—which is even the more urgent and the
more essential of the two, as the withdrawal or inordinate
reduction of the source of heat is incompatible with the
continuance of life, and leads to its rapid extinction—
and to replace the materials consumed in the chemico-
physiological organic processes, if I may be permitted
so to express it, incessantly going on in the body.

The division of foods into heat generators and flesh
formers is, however, by no means sharply defined, as
both mutually partake, in a certain sense and to some
extent, of one another's nature, since the renewal of
flesh by nitrogenous foods is attended with evolution
of heat, and the generation of heat by carbonaceous foods
may be attended with the production of flesh in the
form of fat.

In an excellent little treatise on Household Management and Cookery, which should be in every household of this realm—high and humble—my old friend Tegetmeier adopts the division of food into *albumenoid* and *oleaginous*—the former as resembling white of egg in many properties, the latter as resembling oil in being combustible.

My friend Tegetmeier is unto me a Gamaliel. I crave his kind permission here to transfer to my pages a few general remarks and comments of his on the subject—not by way of an audacious crib, but simply because I consider them most apposite, and feel that I could not express them more simply and clearly:—

"The most important albumenoid articles of our food," says M. Tegetmeier, "are the solid parts of the flesh of animals, the curd of milk, which when dried becomes cheese; the albumen of eggs, gelatin, the gluten of flour, and the curdy matter that forms a large portion of many seeds, as peas, beans, &c.

"The most important of the oleaginous foods are fats, oils, starch, sugar, gum, and the softer and more digestible fibres of plants.

"Many of the articles used as food do not contain a proper proportion of these two kinds of substances, and in economical cooking it is desirable that the defects in one article of diet should be supplied by using it with some other which contains that which is wanting in the first.

"For example, rice and potatoes consist chiefly of starch, and of themselves are bad foods unless combined with fatty and albumenoid matters; therefore we endeavour to use rice in puddings with milk, eggs, and butter, which supply all that is wanting, and it thus becomes a valuable article of food. Potatoes are most useful and economical if eaten with milk, fat meats; alone they are barely able to support life and cannot sustain health and strength. Beans, which are chiefly albumenoid, are eaten with bacon. Bread, which is wanting in fat, with butter or bacon, &c."

The principal object of good cooking is to aid and augment, not to impair and diminish the nutritive action and power of the food to be cooked. Nutrition should always be our chief consideration—superior tastiness of our meals is comparatively of secondary importance. Unhappily, insufficiency of means but too often compels more or less serious modifications of the application of this great principle. The poor cannot command the most nutritive diet; but with a little knowledge of the properties of the various articles of food within their reach, even the poor may be able to feed tolerably well, and maintain the body in health and strength. Cookery that combines nutritiveness and tastiness with economy may be held to achieve the highest desideratum in this important branch of practical Sociology.

PART II.

THE COOK AND THE KITCHEN, LARDER, PANTRY, AND CELLAR, PROVISIONS, ETC.

CHAPTER I.

QUALITIES REQUIRED IN A GOOD COOK.

WHAT may be termed the Cardinal Virtues required in a good cook are, 1—an intelligent knowledge of the art and science of cookery, and of the materials required, with correct judgment in adapting means to ends, and vice versâ; 2—untiring industry; 3—wise economy; 4—scrupulous cleanliness; and, 5—though last not least, sobriety. Of the first of the qualities enumerated here, I shall have occasion to treat in a separate chapter—the next—as it embraces a variety of subjects.

Untiring Industry is an indispensable virtue in a cook. The great Professor Fresenius advises the students in a chemical laboratory never to stand idle a moment, but to be always doing something in furtherance of the work they have in hand, as by intelligently conducting several operations concurrently, instead of idly watching the progress of one, or fixedly awaiting the issue of another, they will secure ample leisure for the performance of a multiplicity of processes, and complete their task within a surprisingly short space of time.

The same advice may be given to cooks. They should always be busy doing something, and that something diligently and well; and they will never seem in a hurry, yet be aye up to the precise time appointed. They should make it a point to train those under their command or guidance to the same habit of intelligent industriousness. Never allow an article you have used to be put by for longer than can practically be helped, without cleaning it or having it cleaned. Never leave your kitchen at night with anything left to be done to prepare it for use next morning. It is the diligent and intelligent employment of time which gives leisure.*

---

* These few words of advice may seem the merest commonplace, and may be deemed supererogatory in a little book like the present; yet my experience has taught me that in but too many kitchens, even of higher pretension, the grossest and most hopeless disorder is, as it were, wilfully cultivated in these respects. I have in some establishments seen the dresser drawers encumbered with miscellaneous collections of articles that certainly had no business there, even to the cook's comb and brush, cold

A *wise economy* is a splendid quality in a cook.
Without it, even the highest culinary genius may come
rather over-expensive.   Only it must be intelligent
economy. What is generally known as attempted cheese-
paring is truly naught but extravagance of the worst
possible kind, and in the most openly foolish disguise.
Never go in for that sort of seeming saving which consists
in the use of cheap materials, such, for instance, as rancid
butter or mutton fat for pastry and frying; or inferior—
miscalled cheap, meat, fish, poultry, vegetables, fruit,
&c. You will always find the best articles the cheapest
in the end.   Let your economy be quantitative *not*
qualitative. Take it for granted that a little of what
is really good will go a longer way than a great deal of
inferior trash. I have more than once seen a pair of
excellent soles reduced to naught in value by frying in
mutton fat, trusting the fat to drain off after, but for-
getting that the delicacy of flavour in the fish could not
well be expected to resist the action of the tallow. Shun

---

cream and puff box, with an elegant assortment, occasionally, of
dirty socks and stockings and pocket handkerchiefs, dish
clouts, and other abominations. I have seen the kitchen knives
reposing in the same box side by side with the dinner sets. I
will not pursue the subject; it is unsavory in the extreme. I
will only add that, in my opinion, the cook who has no method,
system, and order in the arrangement of her kitchen, larder,
pantry, and cellar, robs herself with her eyes open of a notable
portion of most precious time, lost in hunting after things when
they are wanted.

cheap fats in pastry, but always use good butter. It you *must* employ a substitute, take pure lard.

The avoidance of waste in every department of the kitchen, larder, and pantry, is the only true economy. Never let the least scrap go to loss, but always strive to turn every particle of your stores to the very best account. This involves, of course, as an essential condition, the assiduous cultivation of a spirit of order, method, and system. You should always know the exact amount of your stores, &c.; also their kind and quality, as well as the most economical and profitable way to replace or complete them in case of need. Make it a cardinal point in your kitchen and larder management and arrangement to assign a suitable, properly labelled place to everything needed, and to keep everything unchangingly in its proper place. Never throw things down out of hand upon the chance of putting them away after. Your kitchen, larder, and pantry, should never need tidying—they should always be tidy. Never let a saucepan be put away greasy, or with scraps of vegetables, &c., left in it; you will find it great waste of time to have to clean them after.*

Scrupulous cleanliness is equally indispensable. Cleanliness in everything—particularly in personal attire. Vegetables for cooking should be thoroughly

---

* See note on p. 14.

washed and rinsed. Every utensil should look invitingly clean. Even the most lavish use of detergent soap does not always imply scrupulous personal cleanliness. I have often seen cooks wash their hands in plenty of water and soap, yet leave them unclean for want of thorough wiping and drying, and plunge them, still soapy, into delicate messes they were deftly mixing. The hands should always be thoroughly rinsed under a running tap, so as to wash away every particle of the soap. They should then be wiped dry on a clean towel. I have seen *chefs*, of my aquaintance, sprinkle Eau de Cologne or some other scent over their hands when about to work pastry. This always seemed to me an objectionable practice. Personal cleanliness also involves the absence of certain habits incompatible with it—such as snuff-taking to wit, with the untoward effects occasionally attending its indulgence.

I remember—though it is nigh half a century now—when at Lyons, a curious instance of this kind. I belonged at the time to a revolutionary club ; a distinguished *chef*, a M. Poitevin, was a leading member. We were fiercely conspiring at the time, which just then seemed singularly propitious for a promising rising of the second city of the Kingdom. It is generally held that in England alone people require the adjunct of a repast to every act of social or political life. My

C

experience has taught me that other nations also have
the same foible. So a grand banquet was deemed an
indispensable preliminary to the intended grand con-
spiracy. M. Poitevin obligingly volunteered to preside
over the preparation of said banquet, and I readily
consented to act as one of his two chief aids, the other
being a nephew of his, a young man of chaffing disposi-
tion and perversely mischievous. It was while deftly
mixing a delicious Charlotte Russe—with canella and
vanilla in it, and an abundance of the best cream, lots
of yolks, isinglass, plenty of sugar, sponge biscuits
galore, and a variety of jams and jellies, with a sprinkle
of sultanas through the mass—that M. Poitevin be-
thought him of solacing his nose with a huge pinch of
snuff—which, unhappily, along with its effect, went
into the Charlotte ——. I saw it, and so did young
Poitevin.

Lafontaine says somewhere, in connection with some
other human foible—

" *Quand on le sait, c'est peu de chose;*
Quand on ne le sait pas, ce n'est rien."

The second line may no doubt be quite right, but as
to the first I do not believe in it.

So at the banquet I religiously abstained from the
rich Charlotte; so did Poitevin's nephew—which led
to remarks. That young villain audaciously insinuated

the reason of my and his own unwillingness to touch
the delicious dish, by softly humming—

"*J'ai du bon tabac dans ma tabatière.*"

Poor Poitevin's foible being pretty well known, the
"banqueters" put this and that together, and—we did
not conspire that day, which, not unlikely, saved the
July Dynasty for years. The author of "Hours of
Meditation," and of many historic romances and clever
stories, Zschokke, in a wonderful tale of enchain-
ment of causes and effects, traces the participation of
France on the side of Austria in the seven years' war to
the whim of a Paris shoeblack, if my memory misleads
me not. Why should not an unlucky pinch of snuff have
been the cause of the postponement of a revolution?

There is another story told of the great Samuel
Johnson and his *fidus Achates*, Boswell, which runs
on somewhat similar lines—

These two famous men were travelling in Scotland,
it would appear, when they stopped at a small way-side
inn, where the gudewife undertook to provide roast
mutton and pudding for their dinner. Well, the great
moralist strolled casually into the kitchen, where the
mutton was doing brilliantly before a clear, bright
fire, assiduously basted by an urchin of twelve or
thereabout. Now this young "Scot" had his head
covered with a close skull-cap. The inquisitive Doctor

c 2

soon found out that the poor child had, what my late friend
Watkins used to term somewhat gingerly, a *"tineid cepha-
lic exanthema"*—a neat way of wrapping it up. The
Doctor, pondering over his little discovery in connection
with the roasting mutton resolved to make his dinner
entirely of the pudding. The mutton was excellent,
and Boswell went in for it—Samuel abstained, but paid
due attention to the pudding. After dinner, Johnson
laughingly told Boswell of his unlucky discovery, and
to prove the truth of his assertion, had the boy called
in, who presented himself without his skull-cap, in-
genuously informing the Doctor upon inquiry that
"mither" had used it to boil the pudding in. Tableau
—Let us drop the curtain.

Sobriety is a most precious quality in a cook. The
temptations to foster clay-moistening habits are indeed
very great, especially in a large kitchen where much hot
work has to be done. They should, however, be firmly
resisted. Lemonade, water acidulated with fruit
vinegar, and cold tea are much preferable as drinks
even to light dinner ale. I have kitchened with *chefs*
and blue ribbons in France, who drank only water with
piquette and *boisson*—the former a very small nearly
non-alcoholic sourish wine, the latter ditto cider, and
they did very well upon them, and commanded a high
wage rate in the culinary market; their abstention
from drink being held as a pledge and guarantee of

their thorough trustworthiness.   Over and over again
have I also seen in Continental kitchens large basins
filled with cold water in which to immerse the bare
arms and lave the face, which simple expedient will give
refreshing coolness, and to some extent counteract thirst.
The skin may be said to drink in the water, as the
weary and thirsty traveller oftens finds when immersing
his bare legs and arms in some dirty ditch or stagnant
pool by the wayside.   The skin here acts as a filter,
excluding all impurities.

CHAPTER II.

PROVISIONS AND REQUISITES IN KITCHEN, PANTRY, LARDER AND CELLAR.

HERE I must, by way of preliminary, first and foremost crave the indulgent reader's pardon for digressingly straying into the province of social and political economy, with no better excuse to offer than that I have thought deeply upon the subject, and consider its importance in general household management sufficient warrant for its intrusion here.

A good cook should be able to judge by sight, smell, taste and touch of the quality, freshness, comparative value, seasonableness, and general suitableness of the articles supplied by the tradespeople.

I say advisedly by the tradespeople, as, to speak in the words of the late lamented Mrs. Sketchley-Brown, I must confess I do not hold with Co-operative Stores and Societies, which I, on the contrary, look upon as one of the most serious social aberrations and evils of the time. I must crave the reader's indulgence here for a somewhat lengthy digression to make my meaning clear, and state my objections in a frank outspoken way.

The principle of co-operation, in its true application and kept within its proper limits, may be said to form the actual basis of modern society; but falsely applied, and carried beyond its legitimate province, it becomes the bane of society, and must ultimately prove its ruin.

Society, as at present constituted, may be compared to a vast chain of mutually dependent and mutually supporting links. Every class forms a link of the chain, upholding all its fellow links, directly or indirectly, and being in its turn upheld by them. Injury to any one of the links necessarily involves a corresponding proximate or ultimate injury to the whole chain.

It is a self-evident proposition then that the commercial and trading classes form most important links in the great social chain, and that accordingly anything injuriously affecting them must necessarily injuriously re-act upon all other classes.

The merchant and the trader have to live by their commerce or trade. They properly hold the position of middlemen between the producer or importer and the consumer. For their services in this capacity they levy a certain percentage rate of profit on their retail sales. Legitimate healthy competition, which is now-a-days inseparably connected with all pursuits in life, should sufficiently safeguard the consumer against inferior wares and extravagant charges.

Of course, I do not for a moment mean to deny or ignore that there are unhappily monster monopoly markets, and also rings and combinations of certain trades entered into for the deliberate purpose of keeping up artificially, for the most dishonest, selfish ends, the prices of certain commodities, even of those ranking among the first necessaries of life; nor that adulteration of goods of every description has crept in to a most alarming and pernicious extent, or that the most indigent classes of the community are swindled occasion- ally—or even habitually—to a fearful tune. I know all these things are unhappily but too true. But I venture to express my belief that the most efficacious way to put a stop to such gross abuses lies not in co-operative combinations, which, moreover, hardly ever touch the special classes of commodities in which rings may be most successfully worked, but in proper legislation *with stringent criminally penal clauses* extending their protective action down to the lowest strata of society.

Nor let it be overlooked here that the poor man is not likely to ever derive the least benefit from Co-operative Stores. The purchasing power of his scanty wage is in our times following almost unchecked its apparently irresistible tendency to slide downward.

Now, the merchant and trader rank high among the

employers of labour, and a vast body of the community
may be truly said to be almost entirely dependent
upon them.

Our somewhat over-complex State machinery is
worked at a very heavy cost, which the taxpayer has to
defray, and it is upon the merchant and trader that the
chief burden of taxation falls, in our land at least.
Where the golden rule of "live and let live" is the
acknowledged universal law of all classes, society
flourishes. Where miscalculating selfishness is permitted to pervade one or several classes, the consequences
must inevitably prove detrimental to the other classes,
and in the end society perishes.

I know I shall incur ridicule and obloquy, but for all
that I fearlessly give expression here to my deliberate
belief that the deplorable depression of trade and commerce and nearly every branch of industry is, in a
measure at least, more or less directly traceable to the
evil effects wrought by the inordinate spread of the "Co-
operative Stores" system—*Verbum sap.*

I think it was a grievous blunder on the part of our
working men to allow themselves to be tempted to
endeavour to dispense with the intermediary agency of
the merchant and the trader, and to set up as it were
as their own general purveyors.

They must have overlooked the palpable fact that by
just as much as they might succeed in reducing the

prices of articles of consumption, they would also reduce
the means of their principal employers to give them
remunerative employment.

Still, the working man, who has always been an indifferent economist, might plead a most plausible excuse
for his error. He might look upon the saving effected
in his purchases as a notable addition to his scanty
wage. Moreover, in his case the evil had a natural
tendency to correct itself in due course of time; working
men's Co-operative Stores are rarely long-lived.* When
large capitalists and limited liability speculators,
with their natural total disregard of the interests
of others, however vital to the community at large
they may happen to be — for capital and corpora-
tions have no bowels of compassion—strive to accumu-
late in their own hands the most miscellaneous
variety of trades and occupations—selling under the
same gigantic roof, for instance, monster collections of
the most incongruous articles, raw and manufactured
and ready-made — they incontestably inflict a most
serious injury upon the commercial and trading classes.
Still even here there is some slight chance of cor-

---

* Some twelve years ago I attended at the birth of a working
man's Co-operative Store in Strasburg. I had opposed its establishment by every possible argument—in vain. Two years after
I attended at its death and burial. It had done a vast amount of
mischief during its brief career; but the lesson proved effective.

rection, if not of compensation; with so many irons in
the fire, some of them are apt to get cold, and the
Bankruptcy Court may perchance occasionally ad-
minister a salutary warning to likely imitators of such
unwholesome practices. But the most pernicious, the
most detrimental application of the principle of co-operation—lamentably misunderstood and vilely misused—
is that which has of late years obtained in the public
service—civil, and army and navy—and church.

However, upon this part of this incidental theme I
will not dwell here, reserving my comments for another
occasion where they may come in more appropriately
than in the present little work. " Why drag the subject
in at all ? " I think I hear impatient readers exclaim,
" it surely has nothing to do with cookery." Well, to
me it seems it has. One of the most famed authorities
on the culinary art advises her readers first to catch the
hare before proceeding to devise means of cooking it.
Now I honestly believe that if Co-operative Stores are
let go on much farther at full swing, it is by no means
unlikely but that a considerable proportion of those to
whom this little treatise is addressed may find themselves literally unable to catch hares or anything else
in the shape of victuals to cook. This is the reason
for this attempted note of warning and word of
advice.

After this, I will admit, perhaps somewhat unconscionable digression, return we to the requirements of a good cook.

The ability of judging of the quality, &c., of the articles supplied can be fully acquired by practical experience alone—except, perhaps, in the rare instances of cooks to the manner born, in whom the power would seem innate and intuitive. Still even beginners endowed with proper intelligence may soon gain some proficiency in this important branch of the culinary art, by consulting the instructions given and the rules laid down in all really good works on cooking. I take the opportunity here to place a trustworthy cookery book at the very head of the most indispensable requisites in every kitchen. The number of guides and manuals of the kind is truly legion, and it would look invidious and presumptious to single out any one or more of them as specially deserving of public patronage. A word of advice I may offer, however, to the intending purchaser of a cookery book. Do not be guided by the number of receipts a book may contain, but rather look to the introductory part, and see whether the book contains exhaustive instructions in the proper selection of joints, poultry, game, fish, shell-fish, vegetables, fruits, groceries, &c., and in kitchen management in general—fires, ranges, ovens, utensils, &c.

Always strive to adapt your means to the end you

have in view. Suit the size of your pots and pans to
the dishes you wish to prepare in them. This seems
very simple and easy. Yet I have often seen a small
piece of stewing beef, for instance, or a chicken, or a
pigeon, put in pots or pans of comparatively preposterous
size. Nothing is more apt to spoil a dish.

Suit your fire also to your requirements, and strive
to keep it at the proper level—neither too slack nor too
fierce. I have occasionally seen small pieces of meat
put to roast before a fire that might have done for the
largest joints. No wonder that where so little intelligence is shown the roast should turn out dried up and
chippy. Nor will it do to let your fire get over slack.
In this, as in all other things, strive to cultivate the
golden mean. A little intelligent practice will soon
teach you the proper way to do it. The question of
ranges, hot plates, ovens, and boilers lies somewhat
beyond the province of this little treatise. Still I may
say that in a kitchen where large joints are to be
roasted I prefer the old open range, with wide oven,
ample hot plate and hot closets, and boilers at the back
and side, which ought to be made of wrought iron, to
protect them from possible injury from neglect or care-
lessness, especially where they are not self-supplying.
They may be used also as steam boilers for fish,
meat, &c.

I take this opportunity to suggest what I consider

an improvement in ovens—baking or roasting, viz.,—a
wrought iron frame of the inside width and height of
the oven, consisting simply of two uprights, resting on
solid stands, with a bar laid across on top, to hook the
joint to which is to be roasted in the oven. By this
simple contrivance the joint is made to hang free,
surrounded equally on all sides by the hot air of the
oven. The dripping pan—preferably an earthenware
one—is placed underneath for the Yorkshire pudding,
potatoes, &c. ~~I have tried the frame and I have
found it answer.~~ The uprights should have two or
three hooks fixed on them to receive nets stretched
across for doing fish, &c. The cross bar should be
constructed to receive an earthenware or porcelain
cylinder made in two halves to screw together, perforated throughout the lower part. Butter, lard, or
whatever other fat may be required for basting,
according to the nature of the joint, &c., mixed and
worked up into a paste with some flour, to prevent too
rapid melting, is placed in the cylinder, which is
suspended from the bar just above the roasting joint.
This, with clever management, will make the basting
almost automatic. I have tried the frame and have
found it a success. As regards the automatic basting
cylinder here suggested, I cannot speak positively; but
as the difficulties in the way can only be of a technical
and mechanical nature, I think they may be easily

overcome. I think I need hardly mention that in oven roasting, just the same as before an open fire, a strong heat has to be applied at first, to be reduced after.

The perfect range of the future will, I believe, be the gas range—when it shall have received all the improvements of which it is capable, and when electricity shall have replaced gas for lighting purposes, and shall thus have very considerably reduced its present extravagant price. It will then certainly be one of the most economical ways of cooking, as it is the most easily and cleanly managed, the heat being under perfect control. Even as it is, it can be turned to profitable use in many ways; for instance, using rows of concentric rings, two, three, or four of them, with Bunsen burners; every ring with separate gas tap, so as to extend or contract at pleasure the surface of flame, to adapt it to the size of the pots or pans used.*

---

* Many years ago, *eheu!* I used to do a deal of kitchening with the renowned Madame Boileau, a first-rate Parisian purveyor of certain delicate dishes—she "did" for Clericals: *n'est ce pas tout dire?*—such as matchless sturgeon and salmon steaks, rognons sautés au vin de Madère, field lark and field fare pies, and most delicious pastry. The kitchen apparatus was calculated for charcoal, coal and gas. A deal of her frying, stewing, boiling, &c., was done on such concentric gas rings, generally with a Rose burner in the centre. All the raw vegetable offal that would not do for the stock pot, or could not be turned to profitable account in some other way, was put into a special hot closet to dry it, for the purpose of being used as fuel along with coal—a truly economical way of disposing of it.

With a proper gas range you may easily locate your kitchen at the top of the house, with larder and pantry, which is a great advantage in many ways.

Kitchen utensils are, as a rule, amply discussed in cookery books, in some of which they form a truly formidable array, even the smaller sets being occasionally beyond the capacity of a slender purse. Now it is indeed true that kitchen utensils are the tools, as it were, with which cooks have to work. Still all, or even most of them, are not quite so absolutely indispensable as they are made to look. An intelligent cook will, in case of need, find no insuperable difficulty in devising efficient substitutes for many of them, at least, reducing the number of them within manageable limits, and yet will be able to turn out most excellent dinners. It is a trite saying, but none the less true, that a good workman will succeed with indifferent tools, whereas an inferior one will somehow manage to quarrel with the very best set.

There is a story told of a distinguished surgeon who had got all his professional training practically on the deck and in the cockpit of a liner, in the olden days, when the supremacy of the sea was still a hotly contested question. Having, after 1815, retired from the Royal Navy, he presented himself for his proper qualification at the Hall and the College One of the examiners was so ill-advised to ask him how he

would proceed to amputate the leg above the knee.
"With or without instruments?" asked the hero of a
hundred surgical operations, then proceeded to inform the
nettled examiner that he spoke advisedly and without
the least intention to give offence, as he had had to
perform amputations occasionally with a cheese knife
and a carpenter's saw, and yet had made a pretty good
job of it.

I think it was in 1833 that the Prince de Ligne, who
had then just lost his second wife, came to Paris to seek
consolation in the whirl of that gay city. He took up
his temporary quarters in the Rue Richelieu.* One
evening H. H. in passing the Porter's Lodge was
agreeably affected by a delicious smell proceeding from
that generally not over-savory "apartment." He saw
the Concierge, an old woman about sixty, bending
eagerly over a battered old stewpan on a small charcoal
fire, stirring some mess, which evidently was exhaling
the enticing odour. He was an affable gentleman. He
asked the poor woman for a taste of her dish—which he
liked so much that he gave his hospitable entertainer
a double louis, and asked her how it happened that
with such eminent culinary genius she was reduced to a

---

* Six years after, in 1839, I occupied a modest apartment in
the very same house, *au quatrième au dessus de l'entresol.* Here the
story was told me by the Concierge as the proudest tradition of
the mansion.

D

Porter's Lodge. The old lady told him that she had at one time, in her earlier life, for years been head cook to a Cardinal-Archbishop. She had married a bad man, who had spent all her savings, and brought her to ruin and beggary. He was dead now. Although very poor, she added with conscious pride, and no longer disposing of the full *batterie* of an archiepiscopal cuisine, she flattered herself she could manage with a few bits of charcoal and a *méchante casserolle* to cook with the best of them. Next day the Lodge was vacant, the old portress being on her way to Beloeil, the Prince's residence near Mons, in Belgium— where she presided for some fifteen years after over one of the best appointed kitchens in the world.

I tell these two stories here by way of illustrating my meaning, when I say that most excellent work may be achieved with defective tools. Not that I mean to assert, of course, that a kitchen can be properly attended to without a certain set of utensils, only not after the fashion of the subjoined exuberant list; which it must be admitted, however, in common fairness, is deemed indispensable only in a richly-appointed first-rate kitchen :—

Roasting apparatus, meat screens, brass bottle jack, smoke jack; cradle and other spits; patent digester and stew and saucepan digesters; oval boiler; wrought iron stock pots, and assortment of wrought iron and copper kettles; sets of wrought iron saucepans and enamelled stewpans; pans à sauter, or tossing pans; frying pans of various sizes; several large frying pans for fish; sets of patty and tart pans; omelet pans; dripping pans, with basting ladles; cutlet, turtle, Yorkshire pudding, braising, preserving, pickling pans; a number of fish kettles of various sizes; mackerel saucepan; potato steamer; tin Yorkshire pudding dishes of various sizes; soup strainers; fried fish and gravy drainers; mushroom mould, star and scroll fritter moulds, vegetable moulds, pudding, jelly, and cake moulds; sugar moulds; horizontal and hanging gridirons; sets of silver and iron skewers; string boxes; sugar and other canisters; cookholder; weighing machine and balance; meat hooks; colanders, sieves, bolters, tamis and tamines; trussing and larding needles; marble mortars, with ditto pestles; marble slabs, paste boards, rolling pins, and steak beaters; chopping and mincing boards; meat saw, chopper, and cutter; cook's and kitchen knives and forks; salt, flour, pepper, and sugar dredgers; lemon and nutmeg graters; lemon squeezers; fish slice and fish scissors; beef steak tongs; toaster and trivet; salamanders; paste jiggers, cheese toaster, toasting forks; egg slicer and ladles, and egg whisk; iron, brass, copper, wood, and horn spoons of various sizes; freezing machine and ice closet; paste and vegetable cutters; and pig irons, steel egg poacher and egg boilers; fritter irons; herb stand; spice boxes; baking plates; cake tins; pepper and spice mills; seasoning box; *ragout* spoons, ladles of various sizes; sugar canisters, tea and coffee ditto; several sets of carvers — and heaven knows how many other articles besides, all coolly declared to be *absolutely* required by a good cook. Common sense, practice, and experience will soon enable a really good cook to make very large excisions from this list. There are certain things that are, if not absolutely indispensable perhaps, yet most necessary in every kitchen. A good clock, for instance, a correct spring balance for meat, a postal parcel balance for groceries, &c., a small chemical balance, a set of graduated measuring glasses for fluids, a black board to note the time when dishes are put on the hot plate, or in the oven, or before the fire. There is no need to have the eye always fixed on the dial of the clock or on the notings on the board, or to weigh and measure out every trifling ingredient. Still, some little heed had always better be given to these things.* A large chopping board, with raised

---

* Every good cook should ascertain and settle the proper proportions wanted of things. Never go by vague quantities. A handful of salt, for instance, is a vague and misleading direction. I have seen handfuls weighing an ounce and a-half, and handfuls weighing four ounces. A pinch is just as unsatisfactory—varying from thirty grains to a hundred and twenty. An egg may mean from less than an ounce and a half to above two ounces ; a lemon may

ledges at back and sides, with two- or three-bladed
chopper, will also be found most useful; there ought
also to be several smaller chopping boards, for onions,
herbs, &c., so that incongruous articles need not be
chopped on the same board.* A full-sized pastry board,
with proper rolling pin, is one of the most desirable
articles in a kitchen; so is a cucumber slicer. If you
can possibly get a large German slicer, with four or five
superposed sharp-edged blades, set to a narrow guage,
which will answer for slicing cucumbers and cabbages in
the most expeditious and even way, you will find it a
most desirable article. A lemon squeezer, with glass to
receive the juice, is also a most valuable thing in a
kitchen; so is a good mincing machine. A large iron
box, filled with sand, which may be heated to a very
high degree, will be found a great convenience for doing
eggs to a nicety in from three to four minutes, when

---

contain from less than an ounce to two ounces of pure juice. But
that it might look pedantic it would be better to say half an
ounce instead of a tablespoonful, two drams in lieu of a teaspoonful, and to calculate your quantities accordingly. This simply by
way of indication. In this book tablespoonful always means half
an ounce, teaspoonful two drams.

* I have seen onions, parsley, mint, apples, capers, raisins,
meat, *anchovies*, suet, lemon peel, and sweet herbs chopped successively on the same board and with the same chopper-- without
a thought even of an occasional cleaning of either board or
chopper between the operations. There should be separate
choppers as well as separate boards for articles of different kinds.

only the white near the shell will be found firmly
coagulated, the other part being left soft and easily
digestible. If you want your eggs hard-boiled, a few
minutes longer—say eight or ten—will effect the purpose. Only it should always be borne in mind that eggs
are most valuable and nutritious food, containing as they
do all the materials required for the sustenance and
growth of the body. Hardening the white of the egg
greatly impairs its value as a food, especially for young
children and for persons of weak digestion.

In Germany, where the custom of Easter Eggs
flourishes, the hard-boiled eggs, especially those done in
boiling brine, have a trick of lying heavy on the stomach,
and are apt to provide an increase of practice for the
family physician—*Soit dit en passant.*

The sand-bath should be sufficiently deep to allow
the eggs to be completely buried in the sand. Potatoes
also may be splendidly done—particularly middle-sized
ones—in the burning hot sand.*

* It should be a square iron box, say eighteen inches both ways,
suited to a corresponding gas-plate, with several rows of Bunsen's
burners along and across. With a little practice and experience,
the sand-bath will soon be found a most valuable adjunct to the
hearth. It may even enable you to dispense with the use of the
water-bath. A sand-bath heated to the proper degree may serve
even to melt fats, without danger of burning. Omelets and
stirred eggs may be done on it in earthenware fryingpans. To
ascertain whether the sand is sufficiently hot all through, keep
the blade of a knife in it for a few minutes. On removing it from

As regards your water-bath, a few ounces of salt dissolved in it will enable the temperature to rise several degrees—(in a saturated solution even up to 14 F.)—above the boiling point of water—which may sometimes be desirable.

Have nothing to do with skewers and spits; they only serve to make holes in the joint, through which the nutritious juices escape. Use twine or string instead to tie round the joint if necessary.

Never keep coffee or tea in tin canisters, as the tannic acid in these commodities is not unlikely to affect the metal, to however trifling an extent, which will of course react upon the quality of the coffee and tea.

The best way of keeping these and other pantry goods is in glass, porcelain, or earthenware jars. There are certain glass jars in which French plums are supplied to the English market. These generally hold two or three pounds. Their over-lapping screwed covers make

---

the sand, and plunging it immediately into cold water, it should make the water fiz. In smaller kitchens stewpans, some four to six inches deep by six to nine inches in diameter, may be used instead of the large sand-bath.

Many years since I suggested to a Birmingham maker of frying-pans the use of double-bottom plates, with a thin layer of thoroughly ignited sand interposed, which, I expressed my belief, might to some extent protect the frying contents from burning. The gentleman, however, did not see it. Perhaps some other maker may try it now—only mind, this is simply a notion of mine, and that I will not undertake to guarantee its success.

them admirably suited for keeping coffee, tea, and other pantry goods in. They will serve also for herbs. A sprinkling of water, just sufficient to moisten the inside, will keep the herbs perfectly fresh in them for days.

Never place joints, &c., on dishes or plates for keeping. Hang them up in your larder (or cellar, if you have one), from a noosed string tied round the upper end, and suspended from hooks fastened in planks fixed across the ceiling. Do not drive the hook through the joint, for the same reason that you ought to avoid the use of spits and skewers. Joints, &c., ought to hang perfectly free.

Always have a couple of good, sharp, and fine-set grinding-mills in the kitchen, the one for coffee, the other for peas, lentils, pepper, &c.

You will find it convenient also to have a number of muslin bags of various sizes to put herbs in, or vegetables, with which you wish to flavour soups, in cases where their bodily presence in the dish may not be desirable, or where you may wish to conceal the ingredients used. Also a number of nets, with smaller and larger meshes, in which fish and other foods may be put to be done in the oven, stretched across and affixed to the hooks in the uprights of the frame within the oven (see page 28)—dripping, sauce, or stew pans may be put under. A little reflection will soon show the various uses to

which a contrivance of this kind may be put. I simply
make the suggestion.

A few words about pots and pans may not be thought
altogether out of place here. Copper and brass vessels,
carefully attended to, look very nice in a kitchen, and,
if properly tinned, find their uses in many ways. It
must not be overlooked, however, that tinning comes
rather expensive, and that it is inexpedient to prepare
food with acid ingredients in it even in *tinned* brass or
copper vessels. At least, it is always advisable not to keep
the food in them longer than necessary for cooking, but
to transfer it soon to earthenware, tin, tin-plate, or
tinned or enamelled iron vessels. Meat messes should
never be kept overnight in even well-tinned copper or
brass, or, for the matter of that, in iron or tin-plate
vessels, as they are apt to acquire a disagreeable flavour
in them.

In the earlier part of my career glazed earthenware
vessels were to the fore, and I remember well that such
vessels would even stand the open fire. Many an
omelette have I eaten fried in a glazed earthenware
pan. I am afraid the best earthenware now-a-days will
not always stand a fierce fire;* but I know that it will

---

* At the Health Exhibition sets of fire-proof pottery were
shown. I believe they will stand a fierce fire ; but I have not
had a chance of giving them a trial. I have found Chinese
earthen pots suited to the spirit lamp, and to gas and charcoal.

do passing well for the oven or the hot plate. For delicacy of flavour give me a dish done in earthenware in preference over all metal vessels. For slow stewing earthenware is certainly the best, except where the Norwegian stove is used. See below.

New iron pots should always be made ready for use. This is best done by putting the pot to be prepared in a secluded place where children and animals cannot get at it. Boiling water is then measured into it, nearly up to the brim, and oil of vitriol slowly poured over the surface, in the proportion of an ounce per quart of water. The water soon boils again, and keeps boiling for several hours, after which it is thrown out. The empty pot is then scoured clean with sand and ashes, after which washed potato peel is boiled in it, the process being repeated until the last supply of the peel ceases to acquire a blackish tint. After this the scouring is repeated, and the inside of the pot rubbed over with a rind of bacon. Finally, peeled potatoes are boiled in the pot, which are given to the pigs. The article is now ready for use. Rusty pots may be cleaned in the same way.

A so-called Norwegian stove is a most useful and economical article in a kitchen. It consists of a well-made wooden box, with close fitting lid, thickly lined— lid and all—with several layers of woollen felt. An appropriate tin or tin-plate vessel fits neatly in the box. In this vessel the dish to be prepared—say an Irish stew—is heated to boiling on a hot plate, and kept on the full boil for ten or fifteen minutes, when it is rapidly transferred to the box, a thick layer of felt put over it, and the box closed. You may put the box then on a shelf or in a cupboard, and leave it for three or four hours. On opening the box now, you will find your stew or other dish splendidly done, and quite tender. Here you have economy of fuel, combined with good cooking. Even large joints may be done in this most excellent fashion, provided, of course, your Norwegian kitchener be of sufficient capacity.

In a so-called Warren's Cooking Pot (one saucepan placed within another, the outer being filled with water, the inner holding the meat, fowl, ham, &c., without any water), stews and other messes of delicious flavour, tender and juicy, may be done to perfection, as the meat cannot possibly harden from over heating.

I have also seen certain succulent dishes prepared in earthenware (pottery) jars, somewhat after the following fashion: A few slices of fat bacon are put at the bottom of the jar, which is rubbed all over inside with a rind of bacon. A layer of potatoes and onions sliced, chopped parsley and sweet herbs, with pepper and salt, and a little grated nutmeg, is then put in, succeeded by a juicy steak, or a small pork or mutton chop, or a veal cutlet; after which comes another layer of vegetables, steak, and so forth, till the jar is filled, when a few slices of fat bacon are laid on the top. The cover is then put on, and the jar placed in a deep stew-pan, with boiling water, which is kept on the hot plate for two or three hours, according to circumstances.

Do not use metal spoons for salt, vinegar, dishes with citric acid, mustard made with vinegar, or, if you cannot help yourself, clean them thoroughly as soon after as may be, to guard against their being chemically affected. Do not use polishing powders for your plate if you can avoid it. Wash the plate simply in a weak hot (not boiling, mind) solution of an alkaline soap, rinse them in pure warm water, dry them thoroughly in a cloth, and polish them with soft leather. Wooden or glass spoons of appropriate size are the best for salt, mustard, and sour messes. Vinegar will affect horn injuriously, as a horn spoon used long for French mustard will convincingly make clear. The yolk of egg contains sulphur, which readily affects all metals. A horn, wooden, or glass spoon should therefore be used to eat soft boiled eggs with.

The question of preserving eggs is a truly important one. The method most frequently resorted to is to pack them *fresh laid* in a capacious earthenware or porcelain jar, and to cover them over with a thin solution of freshly-slaked lime in water. It is said that this will keep them from summer to winter, and even to

next spring, the only admitted drawback being that the
process renders the shells very brittle. I have tried it
repeatedly; but I must say that—most likely owing to
some fault or oversight of mine—I have found the
process lamentably wanting. After the first month or
so, I have hardly ever found an egg so preserved that
would not run yolk and white together when broken.

My own way is to rub the new laid egg over with a
little sweet Lucca oil or melted lard, so as to close the
pores of the shell. I then wrap a square of tissue paper
round the egg, twirling and twisting the ends up at top
and bottom—the big end at the bottom. I flatten out
the upper twist, pass a needle with worsted through it,
string a dozen or so together in this fashion, and suspend
the strings in an appropriate frame in the larder or
pantry, which must be cool and properly ventilated.
The tissue bags with the eggs must hang quite free,
touching on no side.* I have tried the same way with
lemons, oranges, apples, and pears, with tolerable success.
These fruits may also be kept pretty fresh for a time
by simply wrapping them in tissue paper, and placing
them singly between the twigs of new birch brooms
placed upright against the wall in an airy pantry, or a

---

* Before breaking an egg, hold it before a gas or candle flame,
and try to look through it. If there appear any dark spots or the
least cloudiness, it is a sign that the article is unfit for use.

dry water-tight loft that may be made to serve the purpose of a pantry or larder.

Fresh meat may be kept in winter for close upon a fortnight, by hanging in a cold, airy place—best in a wire meat safe. Never try to preserve joints by rubbing them over with salt, as I have often seen English house-wives do. The salt can only extract the nutritive juice. In summer one of the best ways to keep meat a few days fresh is to roll stinging nettles all round, and sew the joint thus protected up in a thick canvas bag. Keep this in a cellar, suspended from a hook, or laid on a cold stone. An ice cellar is of course the best if you can have the use of one. But on no account lay meat on ice, which imparts an insipid flavour to the meat. Or you may wrap your joint closely up in a cloth kept moistened with malt vinegar. Or you may cover the joint with buttermilk, which must be renewed after two or three days.

However, salicylic acid is a better preservative still than any of these processes.

Pure salicylic acid, which may readily be procured from any respectable chemist, is a white, loose, inodorous powder. In weak solution it is tasteless also. It has not the least injurious effect on the human body, but possesses the very strongest antiseptic properties. To prepare it for use, put about a drachm of it into an empty wine bottle, and fill up with lukewarm water, in which the acid is readily soluble. The solution may be expedited by placing the bottle in warm water. This is the aqueous solution with which meat beginning to putrefy should be repeatedly brushed over in every part, say for about half an hour, after which it is to be thoroughly washed, first in lukewarm then in cold water. This will leave it free from all putrid taste and smell. To prepare a solution of salicylic acid in French brandy, dissolve about a quarter of an ounce of the acid in a pint of the best Cognac. This may be used to keep compotes, preserved fruits, &c.

Fresh strawberries, for instance, intended to be used for a bowl in winter, are washed, let drain, and put into a suitable jar, which is then filled up to the brim with good wine, mixed with the alcoholic salicylic acid solution, in the proportion of about two ounces to the quart. The jar is then carefully tied over with a double layer of properly moistened parchment paper.

Smoked ham and Gotha and Brunswick summer sausages may be easily kept by brushing them over with alcoholic solution of salicylic acid, packing them in perfectly dry straw, sewing them up in canvas, and suspending them free in a cool and airy place.*

---

* This excellent preservative will be found equally useful for a variety of similar purposes. Thus, for instance, where part of a bottle of wine has been poured out, the rest may be kept good by adding a teaspoonful of the alcoholic solution per half bottle of wine.

In my time I have seen fresh joints plunged into
boiling fat, packed in straw, sewn up in canvas bags,
and suspended in the same way in airy cellars, where
they would keep for months. I also remember that we
used to strew fresh killed venison all over with coarsely-
pounded charcoal, pepper, ginger, and pimento (but no
salt, as we knew this would simply extract the best
juices), sew it up in strong canvas, and place it some six
or seven feet deep in the ground, shovelling the earth
back over it, and leaving it for three to four weeks, or
even longer, undisturbed. When dug up the canvas
was removed and the venison washed and rinsed quite
clean, first in lukewarm, then in cold water. It was
then wiped dry inside and outside, anointed all over
with fresh butter or lard, and roasted before a clear
brisk fire. It was delicious.

In an old recipe, dated from the end of the fourteenth
century, burying tainted venison in the earth for three
or four days is recommended as an infallible means to
remove the taint.*

---

* Another way I remember of keeping venison, pork, and wild
boar—particularly rather oldish animals—for several months:
The joints to be preserved are cut into roasting pieces, over which
a little coarsely-pounded charcoal and pepper is sprinkled. The
flesh is incised with a sharp pointed knife, and fat bacon slips,
about half an inch thick, are pressed into the incisions, along with
a few shalots, cloves, and grains of pepper. The joints thus prepared are now given an incipient roasting in the oven, suspended

Vegetables should be procured fresh every day, as most of them lose by keeping, and others can be kept better by the greengrocer than in your cellar or larder. Onions, however, should be artistically tied on a straw rope with string, in so-called hanks, beginning with the large ones at the top, and finishing off with the smaller ones at the lower end. These hanks should be suspended free in a cool and airy place, to let them dry thoroughly. Should frost set in, all you have to do is to gather them in a heap and let them lie there without troubling about them. They will keep well till April, and even May.

Rancid butter may be improved by washing it in water, then working sharp white vinegar through it, taking care to remove the vinegar completely by assiduous kneading and squeezing out. Then salt your butter again, and put it into clean jars or pots, pressing it down firmly. Then insert into every jar or pot five or six sticks of liquorice root, long enough to reach down to the bottom. In a few weeks you will find your

from the hooks attached to the inside frame. When quite cold again, they are packed in a stoneware jar, along with a few onions, pepper grains, juniper seeds, and a sliced lemon, with a modicum of salt. Malt vinegar is boiled, and let cool again. When quite cold it is poured into the jar in sufficient quantity to cover the joints. About an inch of fat is finally poured on. The meat will do for roast, stew, or pastry. Whenever a piece is taken out, the fat has to be re-melted and poured on again.

E

butter considerably improved, as the liquorice root takes off the strong taste. Of course, this process will only do for genuine butter, where the rancidity may be due to imperfect washing. It will not answer with an article adulterated with fat.

Get your salad oil at a respectable Italian warehouse or provision shop. Put two or three tablespoonfuls of absolutely dry table salt to every quart bottle of fresh and sound Lucca, Florence, or Provence oil, and keep the bottle uncorked in a cool place, shaking the contents from time to time together. This will improve the article, and keep it from rancidity.

PART III.

MEAT AND THE PROCESSES OF COOKING IT.

CHAPTER I.

MEATS.

ALL foods—vegetable and animal alike—contain the same nutritive elements, and may, within certain limits, be said to be interchangeable. Yet, as has been intimated already, animal food contains these elements in combinations more or less identical severally with the structures of the body, so that animal foods need not be laboriously resolved into their constituent elements, to be re-formed after into fresh combinations suitable for assimilation and incorporation. It is for this reason that animal foods are more readily and easily assimilated than vegetable foods, and that a larger bulk of the latter is required to provide the same given amount of nutriment as the former. Thus it is that even where vegetable foods contain absolutely

a larger proportion of nutritive matter than animal
foods, the additional expenditure of vital force which
has to be bestowed upon the digestion and assimilation
of the former more than counterbalances this advantage
which they seemingly have over the latter.

Among animal foods the flesh of a certain rather
restricted class of quadrupeds ranks foremost. And
even with regard to these, our concern here is still
further restricted to a very few that fall within the
more immediate scope of our observation in Europe
generally, and in our own country in particular. These
comprise chiefly the ox, the sheep, the pig, and the
goat, with their immature varieties—the calf, to wit, the
lamb, the sucking pig, and the kid—and the pig's wild
congener, the boar. Some would add the horse and
the ass.

As to the humbler of these two, the late Robert Brough
would have it that there were in most human hearts
secret tender chords appealing to a fellow feeling for
poor Ned, and he professed that he looked upon it as
akin to cannibalism to think of knife and fork in
connection with that philosophic animal.

I have occasionally attended so-called " hippophagic-
banquets," with a laudable desire to prove all things;
but I must say the impression said banquets made
at the time on my palate, and left on my mind, could
not well be called pleasing. I will freely admit that

having once forced down my instinctive reluctance to
turn the noble horse into an article of food, I found the
soup and several other dishes tasty and apparently
good to eat; but somehow or other, I always speedily
got satiated. I found soup and meat *too filling*—as
the common saying has it—and with a strong liver
flavour in them, which made me, unlike Oliver Twist,
firmly decline asking for more. So for me the horse
figures not in the list of edible animals; although I am
authoritatively told that there are no physical, chemical,
or rational grounds of any kind for objecting to horse-
flesh as an article of human diet—which would seem to
have been the opinion also, of a certain very learned
German Professor who came over to London in the
year 1851, to see the Great Exhibition, and write a
book about England.

Many great travellers of that period used to take a
few weeks' run over a foreign country, then incon-
tinently to indulge in more or less minute descriptions
of the land and the manners and customs of the people,
of which they knew about as much as the fly does of
the nature, composition and uses of the glass-pane over
which it crawls.

Now, this said learned Professor somehow fell into the
hands of an intimate friend of mine, who with *malice
prepense* took various rises out of him. Among other
trifling sells he took him to the New Cut one night to

a cat's meat shop, informing him that the skewered
slices were the food of the London poor. The learned
man took two skewers home with him. A few months
after his return to Germany his great work upon
England and London and the Great Exhibition made
its appearance in Leipzig. One chapter was especially
devoted to a dissertation upon "How the Poor Live in
London." Of course, the skewer figured in it. The
Professor declared the meat palatable and nourishing,
and wonderfully cheap. He only objected to the
"dryness" of it, and to the scanty proportion of fat.
In a second edition of the book this chapter somehow
was not to be found, somebody having most probably
meanwhile enlightened the author anent the nature
and character of skewered flesh in London.

The bison, the buffalo, the camel, the antelope, the
springbok, the zebra, the kangaroo, and a variety of
other large graminivorous animals that are eaten for
food in America, Africa, and Australia, we pass over
here with this merely nominal allusion.

Certain very low caste people of India and other
lands are said to go in for feeding upon carnivorous
animals, such as dogs, cats, rats, foxes, leopards, wolves,
jackals, and other nasty brutes *ejusdem generis*—a diet
which must be characterized as simply disgusting.

I may say, however, that I have once in my life, at
least, had occasion to indulge in a meal of rats; but

they were barn rats that had always fed upon the choicest grain. I was trapped into eating the mess, but I cannot help remembering that the dish had a most delicate˘ flavour—something between the rabbit and the pigeon—only more alluring than either. Still, I will not upon the strength of this my one and only experience in the matter venture to recommend the proverbial ˙one trial to prove the fact, the less so as I am afraid pure barn rats are rather rare. The French are accused of being occasionally given to mistake pussy for puss, and to turn dear little tabbies into jugged hare. I remember some twenty years ago, when I was boarding in Paris, in the Rue d'Arcole with the renowned Madame Boileau, I got into terrible disgrace once by thoughtlessly indulging in a wretched jest upon this identical subject. Madame had a nice tabby cat, which was a general favourite with the boarders. Pussy one day suddenly was nowhere to be found. Exactly on the fifth day after we had *civet de lièvre* on the table. Well, I jestingly expressed my determination to touch no jugged hare at the establishment until tabby should turn up again. Madame was fierce and furious in her wrath, and one of the leading clerical boarders, *M. le quatrième Vicaire de Notre Dame*, who was, as a rule, a wonderfully mild spoken man, felt impelled by direly impending anti-peristaltic twinges to hurl rather strong objurgations at my devoted head. Now I

was quite convinced in my mind that Madame was
absolutely incapable of juggling or jugging pussy for
puss. Still, as poor tabby was never more seen in the
living flesh, the sting of the vile jest somehow remained
behind, and Madame was hard upon me for weeks
after.

My own bitterest punishment at the time was that I
was self-deprived of my share of the dish, which
Madame was famed to prepare more toothsomely and
succulently than any *chef* I ever knew. I give her own
recipe here in illustration of the intelligent, painstaking
care a first-rate cook will bestow upon the preparation
of a favourite dish :—

Take a fine fresh hare, let it hang four or five
days, then skin and clean it properly, setting aside
the heart and liver. Let it soak two hours in
cold water with an ounce of salt dissolved in it to
the quart. Then wipe it well inside and out, and
lay it in a pottery pan with a quart of new milk poured
over it. Keep it in forty-eight hours, turning it
occasionally. Now pour off the milk, and wipe again
dry. (I cannot exactly undertake to say how the milk
was bestowed after ; but, no doubt, Madame, who
always cultivated a sage economy in her kitchen, knew
how to find a profitable use for it, though she might
scruple to enlighten her boarders upon this interesting
point.) Put the hare back again in the pottery pan,

and pour a quart of herbal vinegar over it.* Leave it in this pickle forty-eight hours, with frequent turning. Wash it now finally in tepid water, wipe it quite dry and rub it all over with a small lump of fresh butter. *Give it a matter of twenty minutes' semi-roasting before a clear fire, keeping it sufficiently far from the glare to prevent the least tinge of hardness on the outside.* Remove it now from the fire, and cut into pieces, dividing the legs into three or four parts, and splitting the head in two. Put the pieces into a proper sized jar, along with a quart of good beef broth with a little salt in it; some savory forced meat balls; the heart and liver boiled and minced; an onion finely chopped, and lightly browned in lard, with a tablespoonful of flour

---

* This should be prepared in June. Put in a stone gallon bottle the following herbs:—Four ounces of fresh plucked tarragon leaves, and two ounces each of fresh parsley, savory, rosemary, lemon thyme, marjoram, chervil, mint and thyme (all unwashed); an ounce of garlic finely chopped, along with the rind of a good sized lemon, in a muslin bag; two ounces of kitchen salt, a grated nutmeg, two ounces of black pepper and cloves finely pounded, also in a muslin bag. Fill up with Orleans vinegar, cork well, and expose the bottle twenty-one days to the rays of the sun. Then decant and filter into another stone gallon bottle, cork well, and keep in a cool place. This herbal vinegar will bear diluting with an equal part of common Orleans vinegar. It may serve also to give a venison flavour to Welsh mutton. It is excellent for ragouts, sauces, and salads. For mutton, hare, or rabbits, the same article may be made use of repeatedly, without detriment to flavour.

worked in, also to light browning; a few mushrooms and some bay leaves. Place the jar now closely covered into the water-bath, and let the contents stew about two hours and a half, which will be found quite sufficient for a young hare. When done add a tablespoonful of mushroom ketchup, one of sauce *piquante* (Worcester sauce), and one of the vinegar in which the hare has been pickled, along with a quartern of good old Port wine, and a lump of sugar.

This recipe may look somewhat complicated, but it is really much less so than it seems. This is one of the cases in which many operations may be carrried on concurrently. And—the reader may trust me—here the game is really worth the candle.

Revenons à nos moutons and the rest of our animal foods.

Beef has at all times, and in all parts of the world, been looked upon by man intuitively as the most nutritious kind of flesh. It was in ancient times regarded as the food best calculated to make warriors fiercest in fight. This is not a scientific treatise, and our space is too limited for elaborate discussion of the composition of the flesh, the proportion of fat to lean, and other highly interesting questions—for which we beg therefore to refer the reader to Dr. Edward Smith's admirable book on foods—an inexhaustible store of information on every point of the subject.

Beef is also the most easily digested meat, two and three-quarters to three hours sufficing for the purpose, whereas mutton takes from three hours to three hours and a quarter.

Lamb, which is an immature meat, is said to be more easily digested than full-grown mutton. Veal and pork are held to be much more difficult of digestion.

With regard to this it may be said, however, that the process of mastication makes a deal of difference. Perfect mastication brings every particle of the flesh under the teeth, and makes the salivary glands fully perform their appointed part in this most important process of life. Saliva is indispensable to digestion. With imperfect mastication there is incomplete secretion of saliva, and the stomach has to work double tides to make up the deficiency. This is more particularly the case with veal and pork, where the underdone and lumped flesh has a tendency to elude the teeth, especially when there happen to be gaps in the incisors or grinders. In such cases cutting the flesh into very small bits, and turning them over and over in the mouth, to give the salivary glands full time to act, will wondrously aid digestion; so that well-roasted veal or pork, properly cut and properly masticated, within the limits set by the state of the teeth, will not take more than from three and three quarters to four and a quarter hours to digest—in lieu of the five hours to five and a half hours claimed by some authorities. Let me remark here that a set of sharp table-knives forms a most important adjunct to proper mastication.

I am sorry to say that I know but too many people who, though gifted with splendid teeth, will persist in swallowing their meals in unchewed lumps, sowing thereby the seeds of *incurable* dyspepsia in after years. I may add from my own dire experience that when some years ago I was irrationally forced to dispose of my dinner within twenty-five minutes, the fierce demon of gastrodynia and gastrorrhœa laid hold of me—and, alas, even to this day I have not done chewing the cud of bitter repentance of my weakness in trying to submit to an unnatural rule.

There is also a popular belief that underdone meat as a rule is more tasty and nutritious, and more easily digested than well-cooked meat. This is simply a superstition, which, like all superstitions, has a tendency to be hurtful. Meat done to a turn is always the most tasty, the most easily digested, the most nutritious, and the most wholesome.

I am quite aware, of course, that there are a great many people who will dissent more or less from this view of mine, and I will not venture to affirm magisterially that I am right, and all the dissenters are wrong. I also fully admit that the other extreme of over-cooking meat is vastly the more hurtful of the two.

Only somehow I cannot help thinking that if we are to eat our meals cooked, they may just as well be properly cooked and well done than be left half raw. I remember some years ago when I was in Paris, Howard Paul invited me to an "English dinner" in the Rue Vivienne, and I shudder even now when I think of the waiter bringing in triumphantly a piece of raw beef, which he placed before us with conscious pride as "*Rosbif Anglais, tout saignant.*"* We sent the choice morsel back, to the intense amazement and disgust of the waiter and of the Maître d'Hôtel. The same remarks apply of course to all other meats, especially to veal, lamb and pork.

MUTTON is more delicately flavoured than beef. It is generally held to be a lighter food, though it is by no

---

* In certain parts of Germany and France a "delicacy" is much patronised by a great many people which is eaten not only "tout saignant," but absolutely raw. A raw steak (as fresh as it can be got) is minced, mixed with finely chopped shalots and parsley, and salt and pepper added to taste. A raw egg is broken over this mess, and the dainty dish is placed before you, with oil and vinegar to add as you may fancy. I do not wish to stand on any one's toes, and there may be people in England inclined for that sort of food ; but I, for my part, must freely confess that I abominate the very sight of it. In Strasburg I used to be invited nearly every day to partake of it, as most of my friends did very freely. There was a Saxon officer who would actually intrigue to get me asked along with him to such raw steak and egg feasts, simply that he might do me the Christian charity to relieve me of my portion—in addition to his own.

means quite so easy of digestion as beef, than which, Dr. Smith truly says, it is less fitted to sustain great exertion, but is rather a food for people of sedentary and quiet habits, including women and children and invalids.

But of all kinds of flesh, PORK is the most universally eaten all over the world—the Old as well as the New— in its various forms of roast and boiled and pickled; cured and dried or smoke-dried ham and bacon; sausages, collared pig's head, &c. In its several forms and dishes it may indeed be said to be the poor man's food, the rich man's luxury. It has maintained its ground through ages—despite religious prohibition and certain most formidable diseases to which it is particularly subject, porcine measles to-wit, and trichinosis, and notwithstanding the indigestibility so widely and persistently imputed to it. The measles and the *trichina spiralis* constitute a very serious danger to the poorer classes, against which they ought to have the fullest protection of effective sanitary regulations.

Concerning the alleged hardness of digestion, I have already had occasion to observe, with proper cooking and carving and cutting, aided by thorough mastication, pork is by no means so indigestible as certain great authorities would have the world believe. Young pork pickled and boiled is nearly as easily digested as beef and mutton. Underdone pork is, no

doubt, very difficult to digest; so is pig's flesh hardened
and shrivelled up by over-roasting, or boiled to rags.
Even that admirable digestive agent, the acid pepsin
glycerin, which is prepared from the stomach of the
pig, may fail to make a proper impression upon such
most unsuitable food. I remember having seen it
recommended somewhere to turn cold pork scraps into
a dainty dish* by frying them in butter or lard! I
have also many times sat ruefully behind a dish of boiled
or roast meat, pork or other, boiled up once more in
curried stock.

Such curries are not good to eat, and often utterly indigestible. True, to make cold mutton or white meats
into a currie is one of the most appetising ways to turn
them to the best account; but it must be done properly,
without giving the meat another boiling, which cannot
but harden and toughen it, and make it indigestible.
The proper way is to cut the cold meat very small.
Take a quart of good stock to two and a half or three
pounds of cold meat. Chop a small onion or two, or
three shalots very fine, and fry in lard to a light
yellowish-brown. Blend two ounces of flour and half

---

* I may remark here *en passant* that there are many cold
scraps that may by proper culinary treatment be made into very
palatable dishes ; but certainly not into "dainty" ones in the
proper acceptation of the term. There are also certain scraps
only fit at the best to go into the stock pot.

an ounce of best currie powder with the stock, add the fried onions or shalots, half an ounce of lemon juice, an ounce of butter, half an ounce of Worcester sauce, quarter of an ounce of Liebig's extract, and forty grains of salt. Put the stock, with the other ingredients, except the meat, in a saucepan over the fire, or on the hot-plate, and let it just come to the boil, with constant stirring. Then add the meat, give the pan a shake, remove from the fire, and dish. This will leave the meat tender, and make a most tasty currie.

There are various ways of boiling the rice for this currie. In the first place, there are two sorts of rice almost indifferently used in some kitchens, though there is a most notable difference between the Indian or Patna rice, to wit, and the Carolina, or American rice. In the former the grains remain upon cooking quite distinct; in the latter they are generally broken up into a mucilaginous mass. As a rule, the Patna is preferentially used accordingly for curries; the American, especially the South Carolina variety, for puddings.

Some high authorities tell you to put the Patna in cold water, let it boil up, drain off the water, replace it by the same quantity of cold water, let it boil up again, strain off the water once more in the colander, stand the latter on the hot-plate, and stir constantly with two forks until the rice is quite tender. By this means every grain will be left distinct.

I remember having watched dear old Thusnelda Irma
many times and often, how she used to put the rice in
a capacious pan in boiling water, keep it five minutes
or so on the boil, strain off the water, replace it with
an equal supply of boiling water, strain off again, and
repeat the same operation once more. I cannot say
how it was, but I think by using the stirring fork with
a very light hand, she succeeded in keeping the grains
distinct, although I believe she used South Carolina
rice. I know the Chinese cooks on board the Shangai
steamers adopt the same mode of preparation. If
I can get Patna I prefer it ; but if not, I philosophi-
cally put up with *old* South Corolina, and though I may
not succeed so well in keeping the grains distinct as the
eminent Blue Ribbon who gave me my earliest lessons
in cookery, my curries, rice and all, are liked indifferently well by my friends. A capacious stew pan
leaving ample room for the swelling of the rice is an
indispensable condition to success in this operation, the
same as in others of a similar nature.

Some ten years ago, when at Strasburg, I made a
rice and fruit pudding for the special delectation of my
friend Schroth, of the Café de L'Espérance, on the Quai
des Bateliers. I will give the recipe:—

Take about a pound of old South Carolina rice, and
four ounces each of prunes, apples and raisins. Quarter
the apples, boil the prunes in an open vessel, and wash

F

the rice and the raisins well. Place a clean cloth dipped in hot water, and squeezed out, in a deep basin, spread it out, lay the rice all round it, and the fruit in the middle, in layers, with a little salt sprinkled between. Add the peel of a lemon chopped, a few cloves, a little cinnamon, with an ounce of pounded loaf sugar. Cover the fruit all round with the rice, and tie the cloth *rather loosely to give the rice room to swell.* Put the pudding cloth thus prepared into plenty of boiling water in a roomy stewpan, placing an old plate under the pudding. Cover the pan and set it on the fire. Boil two hours, and serve. A tasty dish, which may be eaten with roast meat. Gravy, butter melted and browned, and pounded sugar will do for a sauce.

Schroth asked me to tell him how to prepare this pudding. I told him—only omitting the direction about leaving room for the swelling of the rice. He wished to surprise me next day—and he succeeded. We were in the coffee room, when we were startled by an explosion. The pudding bag had burst, and smashed the old plate under it, which unluckily was a bit of rare old china.

Once upon a time a noble English Duke was sent as Ambassador to Paris. He wished to give the *corps diplomatique* there the treat of a real rich English plum pudding. He gave his intelligent *chef* the fullest directions accordingly, even to replacing the water boiling away. Only he omitted all mention of the pudding cloth. The ingredients were calculated for several large puddings. The splendid banquet was served in the lordly dining hall of the Ambassadorial Palace. His Grace, the most charming of hosts, gave the order for the puddings to be brought in. Judge his blank amazement and dismay, and his boiling indignation, when he beheld a procession of eight stalwart cooks walk in, bearing each a huge tureen of some indescribable abominable thick liquid. They had to walk back again, of course, with their precious charges. This shows the wisdom of giving culinary recipes always in full and with all details.

One of the most profitable parts of the PIG is the head, if turned to proper account. Heads from five to seven pounds, including tongue, should always be selected in preference. They may be got at fourpence a pound. To make them into so-called collared head or collar, boil in a good sized saucepan with sufficient water to thoroughly cover the head. Add a little salt to the water. When well boiled the flesh will come easily off the bones. Chop it very fine while hot. Add pepper and salt to taste, and put the mass into a delft bowl or shape, pressing it firmly down with a weight. It will be fit for use next day. The bones may be returned to the stock, which—the fat skimmed carefully off, to be used for frying—will serve to make excellent soup with peas, oatmeal, &c. Oatmeal will always impart an agreeable flavour to every kind of stock or broth. Dredge the meal in with your left hand, and stir with the right, and keep on the fire until the meal is properly burst. Oatmeal with broth is just as tasty as with milk.

I have known some five pounds head and tongue—cost under two shillings—yield up to three pounds of collar, half a gallon of good stock, and a few ounces of fat. In a small household this will be found an economical article of diet.

I crave permission in this place to touch upon a subject somewhat beyond the scope of this little book, yet within the range of the preparation and preservation of food.

Many years ago, when I was Editor of the *Chemical Times*, a valued friend of mine, the late William Maugham, an excellent chemist, suggested to me a new expeditious method of pickling pork. I have more than a vague impression in my mind that I wrote an article on the subject in my journal, to invite attention to the matter. I cannot lay my hand upon it now, but I can recall to my recollection the leading features of the suggestion. A large wooden box is required – say five feet by four feet and four feet—lined throughout with tin, lid and all, so that it may be made air-tight. The front side of the box has a suitable aperture at the lowest part, into which a large tube with tap is screwed air-tight. This tube is connected with an air-pump. The lid has another large aperture, into which another tube with tap is screwed air-tight. This tube is connected with a large tub, placed at an elevation of some 15 to 18 feet above it, filled with the requisite quantity of pickle made with water, spiced vinegar, salt, and sugar in suitable proportions. The meat to be pickled is packed into the box as closely as can practically be done.

The lid is now put on and soldered over air-tight. The tap in connection with the tub is of course turned off, whereas that connected with the air pump is turned on, and the pump set to work. A small steam engine will answer best. When the air is thoroughly exhausted, the tap is turned off, and the connection with the air pump severed, whilst the tap in the lid is fully turned on, whereupon the pickle is drawn with tremendous force into the box, so as to penetrate every part of the pork inside. The apparatus will serve over and over again. I know very little indeed of mechanics—as for the matter of that, of anything else, poor Jacobsen used to tell me—so I cannot say what difficulties may be in the way of the realisation of the suggestion here made. I venture simply to throw it out for the consideration of those who may know more about it; I would also plead in extenuation of any crudeness and

imperfectness of the scheme given that it is drawn
from memory, after many long years.

More recently it has occurred to me that if the plan
is at all realisable, it might be turned to account for the
preservation of meat—simply substituting for the pickle
thoroughly clarified de-albuminated melted fat—beef
fat for beef, mutton fat for mutton, &c. To this end
the box should be lined inside over the tin with woollen
felt, and covered outside with the same material.

The pieces of meat (fresh killed if possible) should be
packed most closely. To ensure the almost absolute
absence of air from the box, some carbonic acid gas
might be let in after exhaustion, and drawn off again.
Provision would, of course, have to be made for this
purpose. I am sadly afraid this suggestion, too, may
incur condemnation as clumsy and visionary; yet, I
honestly think it worth a trial.

Exclusion of air is, at all events, admittedly a chief
factor in the preservation of meat from decomposition.
The non-conducting lining and covering tends to shield
the contents of the box from thermic action. Meat
might be kept fresh in this way long enough, at least
to make it reach our shores undecomposed from the
most distant parts.

I may as well just intimate that I am not altogether
unacquainted with the several processes of preserving
meat by cold; by desiccation; immersion in antiseptic

gases and liquids; coating with fat, &c.; pressure, &c.
But I think the suggestions made here for pickling
and preserving meat differ materially from all of
these.

Of the immature meats, the flesh of the CALF, the LAMB
and the SUCKING PIG, little need be said here. They
are not food in the true and full sense of the word, but
rather luxuries for the table of the rich, and for the
middle and poorer classes on festive occasions. The
premature slaughter of these innocents cannot but act
most prejudicially upon our future chances of meat
supplies. This seems to stand plainly to reason; but
we wilfully shut our eyes to the fact, and go on with
light hearts sacrificing the future to the enjoyment of
the present. What is it that makes war the most
effective check to over-increase of the population?
Why, simply that it mostly strikes down the young
destroying with them the germ of generations upon
generations that might have been but for the premature
extinction of the budding young lives.

England and the United States are the greatest
offenders in this line; for, whilst in most other countries
they allow the poor calf at least some six to nine
months' grace before ruthlessly making it into veal, we
kill our calves occasionally three or four months, or
even only one month old. At Boston, in the United
States, they actually had to pass a law to protect from

slaughter calves less than one month old! And it is
not so very long since that in Ireland they used to kill
new-born calves, and bake them in an oven with
potatoes. They called this dainty "Staggering Bob,"
and it was indeed more than enough to stagger Bob,
aye, and Harry and Jim and Joe too, though apparently
not Pat. This was indeed "seething the kid in the
mother's milk" with a vengeance. The plea advanced
in extenuation of the cruel deed was the scarcity of
provender to rear the young calves. Only—only—I
have heard some Irish friends of mine talk with ecstasy
of the succulent and toothsome "Bob."

The lamb is treated much after the same cruel
fashion, especially when Easter happens to fall in
March. In Holy Russia, where Easter is the great
orthodox Eastern Church festival,* I have seen it

---

* The last week in Lent is kept with special strictness in the
Greek Church. With most devout believers Good Friday and
the day after are black fasts. On Saturday evening the
worshippers gather in the churches, which are left lightless on
that night. Here they prostrate themselves in most fervid
prayer until the first stroke of midnight, which ushers in the
day of the glad tidings that death has been vanquished. Then
all on a sudden the deep darkness all around bursts into a blaze
of innumerable lights. The Chief Priests and the whole congre-
gation after them fall round one another's necks, the one
exclaiming triumphantly "Christos Woskresse!" the other
joyously saying in reply "Istinú Woskresse!"—"Christ has
risen!"—"Ay, indeed He has risen!" Easter Sunday is a day of
universal joy and feasting. In most houses the tables are

placed on the Easter Table roasted whole, side by side with the sucking pig, also roasted whole—both with holy flags stuck in them.

Some English epicures will give the lamb till June, when it is said to be prime. I have gradually come to prefer yearlings, or even two years old mutton. I have a notion it is the mint sauce that makes the dish lamb.

---

literally groaning under the weight of the multitude of good things upon them. Universal brotherhood and all-embracing hospitality are the order of the day. It is an *Agape* of the primitive form. Byron says somewhere, "When I think upon a pot of beer,—but I will not weep," intimating that the thought had a tendency to bring tears to his eyes. Well, when I think upon a "glorious" Easter Feast (*Slava* means glory in Russian), I can barely keep my mouth from watering—after so many long years, too—Eheu!—I was not a semi-abstaining philosopher in those days of my hot youth, when George the Third was King of Great Britain, Ireland and France, and I remember well how I went in for the lamb and the sucking pig. But the latter more especially was deliciously done. Poor little piggie is arranged as for roasting. The brain, heart, and liver are minced and mixed with finely chopped shalot, sage, savory, thyme, and sweet marjoram, and half a pound of good lard. This is the stuffing. A dozen pippins are half roasted in the oven, and put, along with the stuffing, inside the interesting young porker, which is then anointed all over with best Lucca oil, and wrapped in a rich suet paste. Over this a coating is laid of simple flour and water paste, the whole being finally covered all over with a layer of potter's clay. The article is then baked about two hours and a half in a hot oven. The clay and the outer crust (which is generally a little burnt) are removed, and the "sweet kernel" dished.

Halliday came one day unawares upon Fred Lawrence, who was devouring a dish of roast pork, with a modicum of veal stuffing by the side of it. "Ah! eating pork, Lawrence?" cried the P. P. of the Savage Club. "Pork be hanged," was the reply. "It has been baptised veal since I sat down to it. Don't you see the stuffing?"

When I talk of mint sauce I do not mean the wretched mess of a few imperfectly chopped dry mint leaves swimming about in a sea of malt vinegar, with a few grains of raw sugar dissolved in it, which one gets in some London dinning rooms, and occasionally even at private tables, and which has its admirers, too, among some *chefs* and blue ribbons, who coolly tell you that half an ounce of moist sugar will do for five fluid ounces of malt vinegar. I recommend the following recipe:—Take a sufficiently large bunch of fresh green young mint to fill, when finely chopped, two to three tablespoonfuls. Chop the rind of a good-sized lemon very fine, and add it to the mint in a sauce tureen. To four ounces of best French vinegar add one ounce and a half of fresh lemon juice, and dissolve in this as much finely powdered best loaf sugar as it will absorb. Pour the solution over the mint in the tureen, and let it stand an hour or so. Try to get your mint clean that it may not need washing, which tends to take the freshness off. If needed rinse the bunch under the flowing tap, shake it, and let the water drain off on a

clean dry cloth. I have a notion that with this sauce
even four years old mutton, properly roasted, may be
made to taste something like lamb. At least there can
be no harm in recommending a trial.

Some years ago I went to dine one day at the
" Portugal," in Fleet Street. The fancy took me to order
caper sauce with my roast mutton. The waiter looked
amazed, and instead of bringing the caper sauce
ordered, he brought down the proprietor upon me, who
very politely asked me whether there was not some
mistake, and that it was *boiled* mutton I wanted. I
told him with equal politeness that I wanted roast
mutton and caper sauce, and asked him whether he
saw any moral objection to it. He went away shaking
his head. A few weeks later I happened to look in
again, when the proprietor came up all smiles to tell
me, to my intense gratification, that he had tried caper
sauce with roast mutton, and that he found it a great
institution.*

---

* After all there is no great incongruity in taking caper sauce
with roast mutton. It is certainly not so irrational as Lord
Byron's *hospitable* invitation to poor Joe Grimaldi to take soy
with appletart, because, as his Lordship pleasantly observed, soy
was good to eat with salmon—why not then with appletart? I
cannot help thinking but that on this occasion the immortal poet
ran the clown very close in his special line.

Mustard is as a rule looked upon as the proper condiment to
be eaten with roast and boiled pork, ham, and boiled beef—
certainly not with mutton, roast or boiled. Many years ago

Dr. Julius Fancher, a German gentleman of French extraction, who afterwards became a member of the Progressist Party in the Prussian Chamber, acted in London as private Secretary to Richard Cobden. I knew him intimately at the time. His great boast was that he was free from the least tinge of eccentricity. Well, one day I had invited him to a roast shoulder of mutton. I saw that he was fidgety and glancing about in every direction. "What is it you are looking for?" I asked. "Where is the mustard?" he replied. "I cannot eat mutton without mustard."

It was in the earlier days of the Savage Club when its local habitation was the Lyceum Tavern, then under the management of Mrs. Spielman and her daughters. I was mixing a grand salad. Finding that the oil ran rather short, I sent Old William, the waiter, down to the bar with a polite request for an additional supply. The young ladies obligingly sent up a flask, from which I, being in a hurry, proceeded at once to make up the deficiency, when—alas, too late—my nose revealed to me and others the sad fact that it was the ladies' hair oil which I had used. I was mercilessly chaffed, of course, by none more than by my friend Tegetmeier, who has always been my rival in salads and grogs. The stupid old waiter had asked for "more oil," and the ladies had understood "hair oil."

A story is told of a young lady in Germany who had got married chiefly upon her supposed skill in pastry. The misfortune was that it was the mother who was the real cook, the young lady being well-nigh innocent of all and everything pertaining to the kitchen. She trusted however her deceit would not be found out, as she was firmly resolved to turn over a new leaf, and to be guided in her culinary efforts by a good cookery book. So when after the honeymoon the young couple settled down to the sober business of life in a home of their own, with a single servant—a raw country girl ignorant of everything—the young bride entered upon the study of cookery with a will, and for a few days she managed pretty well. The husband, wishful to show off his charmer's brilliant talents in the pastry way, invited a couple of friends to dinner, and begged his little wife to make a mixed first-rate fruit pie, such as he had often tasted at her father's table. Well, the cookery book was duly consulted, and everything was done as directed—that is to say, everything down to the bottom of the page where the last words were "two teacupfuls," the first word on the next page being "wine," followed by "a lemon sliced, the peel of a lemon grated, and a little cinnamon." Now, as mischief would have it, the two leaves stuck together, and the first words on the third page, referring to a meat pie, were "good gravy, a tablespoonful of chopped shalots and mushrooms, a teaspoonful of chopped sweet herbs, two of salt, and one of mixed cayenne, cloves and piments." Well this rather startled the young lady, but her notions of things in general were altogether rather vague, and she had often heard her mother say that fine cookery consisted chiefly in the harmonious blending of apparently incompatible ingredients. So the pie was made according to these directions, and it certainly *was* a dainty dish to set before her husband and his guests. And when the pie was opened, and tasted, there was something like a scene. It ended in a contrite confession, and the young lady did not venture upon pastry again for some time after.

CHAPTER II.

It has been said already in a former part that the principal object of good cooking is to aid and augment, not to impair and diminish, the nutritive action and effect of the food to be cooked. The chief requisites to achieve this object are that the cooked food should be easy to chew and easy to digest; the achievement of the former goes a very long way towards that of the latter.

In southern latitudes flesh is held to be the most tender and juicy if eaten immediately after the animal has been killed. It is reported of the Abyssinians that at their great feasts they love to cut the flesh from the living animal, to broil and eat it on the spot—which is truly horrible to contemplate. When the death stiffness sets in, the flesh gets less tender, and more difficult to chew and digest, which of course must tend to impair its nutritive qualities. It is in this stage, more especially, that it may be improved for cooking by cutting it into thin slices, and beating it across the cut ends to break the fibres. After a time—shorter or longer according to the temperature—the stiffness relaxes, and the flesh enters into the incipient stage of decomposition, which tends to soon render it soft and tender again. It is at this stage that in our latitudes it is fittest for the processes of cooking. The few general remarks I have to make upon these processes, some of which have moreover already been touched upon incidentally, may be briefly summarised under the several heads of *Boiling, Stewing* and *Braising;* and *Roasting, Baking* and *Frying* and *Broiling.*

I place BOILING, STEWING, and BRAISING, first, because the processes of boiling flesh are by many able judges considered to be more simple, more easy, and more economical than roasting, &c. Within certain limits, I am much inclined to be of the same opinion.

Every process of cooking flesh is unavoidably attended with a certain loss of weight, which admittedly is larger in roasting, &c., than in boiling, &c.,—that is to say, of course, if every product of the process is properly utilised.

BOILING has two very distinct, widely different objects in view, to wit, either to extract part of the juices, whilst attending to the tenderness of the cooked flesh, or to retain, as fully as practicable, the gravy in the meat.

To effect the former purpose put the joint in *cold*

water, place the saucepan on the fire, and raise the heat slowly to the boiling point. Remove it now at once to a much more moderately heated part, and let it simmer on until the joint is properly cooked—as in this case, both the meat and the broth are eaten, there cannot possibly be much real loss of nutritive matter.*

Where, on the other hand, it is desired to retain the largest practicable proportion of gravy in the meat, the joint is put for about fifteen minutes in boiling water. The exudation of the juices proceeds chiefly from the cut ends of the soft fibres, and ceases as soon as these ends have become hardened from the coagulation of the albumen. Now albumen coagulates at a temperature very much below the boiling point of water (at 120°). A quarter of an hour's immersion in boiling water, is therefore, amply sufficient to prevent—or nearly so—further exudation of nutritive juices. But the contact with boiling water must not be continued beyond fifteen minutes, after which the saucepan has to be drawn

---

* Anent the boiling of hams, Mr. Tegetmeier tells us that at the large ham and beef shops in London, where the meat is generally very tender, the hams are always placed in cold water in a copper, under which a small fire is made, which raises the water very gradually to the boiling point. The moment this is accomplished the fire is raked out, the copper covered over, and the hams are allowed to remain in the water until it is nearly cold. In this manner they are several hours in cooking, and never are permitted to reach the boiling point. This mode of cooking makes the flesh exceedingly tender, and guards against loss of fat.

back from the fire, and the cooking continued at a low heat until the joint is thoroughly done.

When you carve a leg of mutton done in this fashion, the gravy gushes forth the moment the knife is put into the joint, and lusciously spreads all over the dish.

A leg of mutton properly boiled, is in truth, one of the most delightful dishes that can be set on a dinner table. There is only one not unimportant drawback to it, as my friend Draper observes, to wit, the difficulty of making a palatable meal of the part left over, where the family is too small to dispose of the whole at a sitting. A currie will of course do, but then all people do not like curries. I think cold boiled mutton will bear braising, particularly if mixed with some pieces of fresh mutton. Of course, this requires a good braising pan, with close fitting lid. Lay at the bottom of the pan a few slices of fat bacon, on which spread a thin layer of coarsely chopped suet; add pepper and cloves whole, a few small pieces of ginger, a Spanish onion cut in thick slices, a few bay leaves, sweet herbs and parsley, and a bit of celery. Place the meat on this cut up in large pieces—the fresh meat first and last, the cold boiled in the middle (a little salt should be sprinkled on the meat); finish up with slices of fat bacon. Pour gravy over it just barely sufficient to cover, put on the lid tight, set the pan on the hot plate, fill the hollow cover with live charcoal or red hot cinders, and let it do slowly. When

G

done, strain the gravy through a strainer, skim off the fat, and add a spoonful of Worcester sauce and a squeeze of lemon to the skimmed gravy. I have a notion this will be found a tasty dish, and a simple way of disposing profitably of the scraps of cold boiled mutton.

STEWING is a modification of boiling, which M. Tegetmeier and other high authorities on the science and art of cooking consider more advantageous and economical than the latter process. I incline much to the same opinion—except always, of course, in the matter of *boiled* leg of mutton, as expatiated upon above.

In stewing, the meat should, if possible, be placed in an earthen vessel, with a small quantity of liquid, as a rule, and exposed to the long continued action of a very moderate heat, which naturally tends to soften the fibres, and to make the flesh of old animals, and tough, sinewy joints, easy to chew and digest, thus enabling a good cook to turn the coarsest and cheapest meat into savoury and nutritious food, very little, if indeed at all, inferior to prime joints.

BRAISING is simply a modification of stewing, which has been sufficiently described under BOILING.

The processes of ROASTING and BAKING have been incidentally touched upon already; still, a few words may be added here in reference to the former.

In so far as small joints are concerned, roasting is certainly not the least wasteful process of cooking, nor even always the most satisfactory in its product. The heat being less evenly and gently applied, as a rule, in roasting before a free fire, the outside is apt to become overdone before the inside is sufficiently cooked, and the waste of the juices extracted is greater than in boiling. And this loss cannot well be guarded against by the action of boiling water, as this might injuriously affect the roasting. In my earlier days I have seen joints dipped a few minutes in boiling fat, to prevent exudation of the juice from the cut ends. I am afraid, however, there are practical difficulties here that cannot be disregarded. The only way which is left open is to bring the joint, protected by a Dutch oven or screen, quite near a sharp, brisk fire at first to induce coagulation of the albumen all over the surface, then to remove it to a proper distance for roasting. However, this answers the purpose only imperfectly at best.

Now ROASTING happens to be the favourite process of cooking meat in this country—and there is certainly no other land in the world where the process is so thoroughly understood as a rule, and so perfectly performed. I have known first-class French *chefs* fail in the roasting a leg of mutton, for instance, before an open fire, in the way in which a second rate English plain cook will brilliantly achieve the task, and think nothing of it.

An old friend of mine—now no more—a first rate cook
in his time, who had been steward many years on
board a Rhine steamer, established several large dining
rooms in London. His kitchens were admirably de-
signed and appointed. In one, which ·I knew more
particularly, he had engaged a *chef*, a *sous-chef*, a first
and second cook, two scullery and two vegetable maids.
He did not like to change his servants, so his engage-
ments were always made slowly and after due reflection
and deliberation. When he had to engage a cook he
declined looking at testimonials vouching for the candidate's skill in soups, entrées and pastry, but he
invariably asked, "Can you boil an egg? Can you boil
a potato? Can you properly broil a steak and a
chop?" And, lastly, "*can you roast a leg of mutton?*"
If she came up to these requirements (of which he, of
course, exacted practical proof in his presence) she was
sure to be engaged by him at liberal wages and under
easy general stipulations that made it well worth her
while to try her best to keep her place. The *chefs*
and the other members of the kitchen staff being
selected upon the same principle of crucial tests in
some of the leading branches of their special province,
the result was, of course, that the business prospered.

BROILING is one of the most delicate processes of
cooking. It deals only with smaller pieces of meat,
such as chops or steaks, which are exposed to a hot

open fire, and by rapid repeated turnings (best with proper broiling tongs) made to retain their juices. *No thin pieces should ever be broiled,* but only thick, fleshy pieces. No fork should ever be stuck into them, nor should they be cut with a knife, as some cooks are but too apt to do, just to see whether they are done sufficiently. The fire must be perfectly clear, and as free as possible from licking flames. A horizontal gridiron placed over a large clear fire is the best to broil on. A hanging gridiron will, however, answer the purpose. The removal of all fat from the chop or steak will greatly facilitate the process, and improve the result. You may sprinkle your steak or chop with a little pepper, but always reserve the addition of salt till the meat is done.

By way of example : Have three or four mutton or lamb chops properly cut and trimmed, removing the fat; beat them thoroughly with the steak-beater; dip them in melted butter, sprinkle them with a little pepper and salt—(which here can do no harm, as the coating of butter protects the meat)—and roll them in pounded plain biscuit. Then place them on the gridiron over a fine clear fire, and give them eight minutes broiling, four minutes on each side, turning them rapidly every two minutes. They should be served piping hot.

I beg to observe here, incidentally, that my friend Draper suggests to me a practical way of collecting on bread the drippings from chops, steaks, ham, bacon, &c.; broiling or toasting on a hanging gridiron before an open fire, by simply placing underneath the gridiron, on a plate, a round of bread well toasted on the lower side. The drippings will soak into the bread, the semi-carbonization of the lower side preventing their passing through.

FRYING is the least desirable method of cooking meat. A late lady friend of mine, who was no mean authority on culinary matters, used to express a devout wish that every fryingpan cost a guinea. I must confess that I feel often tempted to echo the wish, more especially now when iron and imperfectly enamelled pans have taken the place of the good old earthen pan, in which the fat was easily kept from overheating, and meat fried in it from hardening. But even in those "halcyon" days of the long past I had a notion that the use of the fryingpan should be confined as much as possible to fish, omelets, pancakes, onions, potato chips, and similar eatables. To do omelets and pancakes properly requires some judgment and skill.*

---

* Regarding pancakes, a friend of mine, Mr. Linford, of Hull, an eminent chemist and distinguished gastronomist (chemistry and gastronomy are kindred pursuits), writes to me:—"PANCAKES —All books tell you to be very particular that your batter be mixed quite smooth. All books are wrong. Mix your eggs—well beaten—with your milk, scatter in the flour, just stir it round, and dip out and pour into the pan at once. There will

Eggs fried in a pan are more or less apt to be indigestible—generally more so; which is hardly to be
wondered at, seeing that the process tends to thoroughly
coagulate and harden the albumen. In frying fish,
more especially the dainty whitebait, tender sole, and
others of the same delicate nature, always use—if
you possibly can afford it—good butter, pure lard, or
sweet salad oil. Beef dripping will do à la rigueur;
but mutton fat will not—at least not for fine palates:
though I confess I know a gentleman who always fries
his fish in mutton fat. But then he is a splendid cook
—one out of a thousand; and I have reason to know
that he uses only the fat of young sheep, which he pre-
pares by keeping it in fresh water for twelve hours,
then chopping it fine, and boiling it with a small cupful
of milk over a gentle fire—in an open pan—with frequent stirring, until the fat looks quite clear. This is
the German way of rendering mutton fat. Under any
circumstances, good sound mutton fat is vastly preferable to bad butter and to the fatty abominations that
are palmed upon the public as "butter." I will venture

---

be numerous small nodules of flour not wetted. The air
imprisoned therein when poured into the pan expands quickly,
and converts each nodule into a bubble, so that your pancake is
like fried froth. Try it." [I *have* tried—and I must say I never
tasted such wondrously light pancakes before.] "Of course I
need not tell you that the temperature of the pan is of the greatest
importance."

to state over again here my firm conviction that the use of inferior articles in cooking is " wasteful " economy, if the contradiction in terms may be permitted to pass. It need hardly be added here that there should always be sufficient fat or butter in the pan to cover the frying fish, &c.

After use, always scour your pan (as indeed should be done to *all* pots and pans, &c., used in cooking processes) thoroughly, wipe it quite dry, and hang it up in a place free from humidity. Before using it again, set it on the fire with cold water. When the water is hot, wash the pan well, and wipe it quite dry. I have but too often seen fryingpans—and stewpans, too, for the matter of that—put away unwashed; and I have seen omelets and pancakes done in pans lately used to do herrings, or bloaters, or sprats, or some other strong-scented delicacy. Have *at least* always a separate pan for fish, and one for pancakes and omelets. Enamelled fryingpans are cheap enough even for slender purses.

This seems a convenient place to say something of a palatable dish of cold scraps, requiring the use of the fryingpan—so-called *boulettes*, a kind of flattened forced meat-balls. These may be made properly only of scraps of *underdone roast* beef, pork, and veal. Mutton will not do, nor will scraps of boiled meat. The roast beef scraps intended for *boulettes must* be underdone, as the subsequent frying would otherwise harden and toughen the meat; and *boulettes* should be easy to masticate. Pork and veal scraps may be used if a little more done (though not too much, mind). If you have scraps of the three meats, take equal quantities of each, say half a pound, for instance—more or less, of course, according to supply or requirement. If you have only pork, get the same quantity of beefsteak, and broil it to the same degree as the pork is done. The veal may be omitted. If only beef, get the same weight of pork chops, and broil them in the same way. If only veal, get both the steak and the pork chops. In case of need, you may substitute for the pork raw ham and fat bacon, in the proportion of two parts of the former to one of the latter. If you have only lean meat, add fat bacon—say four ounces to a pound and a half of meat. Carefully remove all sinewy and skinny parts. Mince the meat very fine (best in the mincing machine). Chop about three ounces of onion or (better) shalots, a bunch of savoury herbs, and two ounces of parsley, very fine. Add the peel of a lemon grated, a teaspoonful of salt, half a tablespoonful of Worcester sauce, and the juice of half a lemon—pips taken out. Mix with the minced meat; add two raw eggs, yolks and whites, to bind the mass, and make into balls of about two ounces each. Flatten the balls neatly with a beater to about half an inch thick, and fry in lard to a nice light brown on both sides. Some recommend to give the onions, parsley, and

herbs a preliminary turn in the pan, which may be an
improvement. The *boulettes* should be served with
mashed potatoes. An agreeable meal, with a good
salad.

SALTING MEAT.—In his admirable "Handbook of
Household Management and Cookery," M. Tegetmeier
comments adversely on the process of salting meat
before cooking, which is so largely—it may almost be
said universally—adopted in this country. As I most
fully agree with M. Tegetmeier on this physiologically
and economically most important question, I crave
the author's kind leave to transfer to my page his
most excellent remarks on this subject, that my own
diffident opinion may have the support of his high
authority:—

"Salting meat is in most cases a very wasteful process; salt when applied to fresh meat extracts a very
large proportion of the nutritious juices of the flesh, and
at the same time hardens the fibres and renders them
much less easily digestible. The brine that runs from
salted meat contains so much nutritious albumen that
it becomes nearly solid on being heated, and as there
are no means of extracting the salt, it is necessarily
wasted.

"The salting of meat before cooking is an English
prejudice which is not followed in any other country;
nor is there any good reason why beef and pork should

be salted before boiling, and mutton and veal boiled without salting. The plan followed on the Continent, of slowly stewing a joint of beef without first salting it, yields a much more nutritious, tender, and well-flavoured food.

"In cases where it is necessary to preserve meat, as on shipboard, salting may be useful; but health cannot be preserved for any length of time on meat from which the most valuable part, the nutritious juices, has been extracted by salting.

"In the case of very fat meats, as bacon, salting is not objectionable, as in them the most valuable constituent is the fat, which is not injured by the process.

"In the case of ham a peculiar flavour is produced during the process of salting which is highly esteemed; but it should be remembered that the value of the flesh of ham as food is much, very much less than that of the meat from which it is produced."

I was told some time since that a process has been invented to extract the salt from brine. Having had no opportunity as yet of practically testing this reported invention, I cannot speak of it from personal knowledge and experience. If the process is really effective in taking the salt out of brine, one of the leading objections to the salting of beef and pork before boiling may no doubt be considerably modified thereby.

The statement that the English mode of salting meat

before cooking is not followed in any other country is, perhaps, a little too absolute. In my early days I have often seen our own cook salt and pickle fat joints of beef and pork. I remember she never would use saltpetre either for simple salting or full pickling.

I cannot call to mind at this distance of time what she used for a substitute, or how she managed to preserve the colour of the meat. But I remember quite well her favourite pickle. She made this of two quarts of water, ten ounces of salt, one and a half ounce of brown Muscovado, two and a half ounces treacle, half an ounce each of cloves, mace, and pepper, two ounces of Orleans vinegar. This mixture was boiled half an hour, with careful skimming, allowed to cool, and when quite cold poured over the pickling flesh. The quantities here given were calculated for ten pounds of beef or pork. The meat was left eight to ten days in this pickle. For use, it was set on the fire in boiling water, to prevent the escape of the juices. The same pickle, boiled and skimmed again, was used once or twice more. To my recollection, she never salted or pickled any but fat meat.

A few words on EXTRACTS OF MEAT, and on the so-called CARNE PURA, or *flesh-meal*, or *meat-powder*.

Extracts of meat are prepared by evaporating the flesh of animals nearly to dryness. They are largely imported into this country from Australia. It is said that thirty-two pounds of fresh meat have to be boiled down to produce one pound of Extract. I feel much inclined to hold this to be a notable exaggeration. However, this matters but little after all, but what matters much is that the Extract, such as it is sent into the market, is reft nearly of all the really nutritious part of the fresh meat, very little being left in it beyond the flavouring matter and the salts, which will serve, indeed, to impart to beef-tea, &c., an agreeable flavour and a rich colour; but with nothing solid behind. Still, Meat Extracts are very useful, as they serve to improve— mind, not strengthen—stock, gravies, soups, curries, sauces, &c., and stand just a degree or so above mere condiments, inasmuch as they retain some little nutriment. Unfortunately the price of even the cheaper sorts is extravagantly high.

The *Carne pura*, as it is termed in the trade, or *flesh-meal*, or *meat-powder*, comes from South America, where vast herds of cattle graze on the prairies, or pampas. There the fresh flesh is evaporated to dryness, then ground to powder. I have been assured that *Carne pura* is a very superior article, and considerably more nutritive than Australian Meat Extract. A small sample was sent to me from Germany—where it would appear the American product is getting as popular as the Australian is here—and I was asked to give it a trial. Well, I have done so honestly; but whether it was that the sample had been badly selected, or from whatever other cause, I failed to find the article any way superior to Meat Extract. Neither of them will make good beef-tea--not even with the aid of bones.

PART IV.

POULTRY AND GAME—FISH AND SHELLFISH—MOLLUSCS AND TURTLE.

OF course it is not in the design and scope of this little book to discuss these classes of foods in detail. They may be dismissed, for the most part, with mere nominal references and brief. allusions. Still, a few cursory general remarks and hints here and there may not be deemed altogether out of place.

CHAPTER I.

POULTRY AND GAME.

WITH special reference to English cookery this class comprises chiefly the common fowl, turkey, goose and duck, with their wild congeners; teal, quail, widgeon, waterhen, grouse, moor-game, black-game, heath-game, partridge, pheasant, plover, guinea-fowl, woodcock, snipe, capercailzie, and a variety of other birds, which are eaten in England mostly roasted or baked in pies. I am sorry to say that we have to add the " sweet singer of the Empyrean," the Ettrick Shepherd's Bird of the Wilderness—the lark—along with the thrush, the blackbird, the fieldfare, the finch, and other melodious warblers, to the list of birds eaten in England, roasted on skewers or baked in a pie—which seems a crying shame.

There was once a monstrous glutton, a veritable " opprobrium humani generis," Aulus Vitellius by name, whom the sweet will of a rebellious soldiery imposed upon degenerate Rome ·as ruler over the vast Empire. This beastly brute used to take emetics to enable him to gorge three or four dinners a day. Within the short space of eight months that he was permitted to soil the Imperial Seat he squandered some forty millions sterling—computed upon the actual value of money—upon his table! At one of his banquets two thousand rare fishes were served up along with seven thousand birds ! On another occasion he had a huge dish made of thousands of tongues of birds, especially singing birds. The bearing of this incidental digression lies in the application of it, as great Captain Bunsby used to say.

Well, well ! England is certainly not the worst

offender in this way. On the Continent they seem to go in *con amore* for eating small singing birds, particularly the lark, the fieldfare, the finch, and the thrush. In France, I am told, they add the gentle robin to the list of edible birds.

For the matter of that, it is averred that all classes and species of birds are eatable, and eaten somewhere or other; even the carnivorous and carrion birds, which it would appear the low caste natives of India will occasionally devour with great relish, when they themselves are more than half starving, I should think. But the wholesale slayers of the sweet songsters of the sky cannot plead this excuse in extenuation.

The pea-hen is still occasionally eaten in England. I have heard gourmets warmly extol the delicate flavour of the flesh—between that of the chicken and the pheasant.

As for the peacock, the pride of the gallinaceous tribe, its beauty surely should exempt it from spit or crust. And in England it is pretty nearly so, though it is said to be served still as a rare dish on rare occasions.

But our Continental friends are restrained by no scruple from roasting this glorious bird on the spit or baking it in a pie.

I had always managed to steer clear of what I con-

H

sidered the meanness of abetting the cruel slaughter of
the peacock by joining in the eating of it. Alas, for the
inconsistency of man !

Some eleven years ago I was travelling in Germany.
At Elberfeld a friend invited me to dinner at his
mansion. It was a superb banquet that might have
rejoiced the heart and palate of the most fastidious epicure—certainly it rejoiced mine. Only it was with an
involuntary shudder that I·saw placed on the table a
large pie dish, with a splendid peacock's head stuck on
the top, to show it was that noble bird that was
inside.

Well, I could not, in the commonest courtesy, decline
to partake of the pie, the less so after the graceful
intimation made to me by the gracious hostess that
the pie had been specially made for the occasion
with her own fair hands. Well, well! to my shame
be it confessed, I found the dish delicious, so much
so, indeed, that it required a stern resolution on my
part to leave off in decent time. That I did not
even feel any very acute pangs of conscience may
be gathered from the fact that I asked the lady for
the recipe, which she kindly gave me. I remember
it pretty accurately, having repeatedly had to write
it out for friends. On one occasion I had even to
try it practically ; but then the bird had been killed
when I was asked, so that my consent or refusal could

no longer affect it.[*] I consider that if this noble bird is ever to be eaten, it should be done in the most tasty fashion; so I venture to transcribe the instructions here as I recollect them :—

Take a young peacock. Let it hang three or four days in a cool, airy place. Pick it to the head, which cut off to ornament the top of the pie. Draw and clean the bird, washing it thoroughly. Then rub it all over, inside and out, with fine table salt, mixed with an ounce of pounded pepper, pimento, and cloves, and grated nutmeg. Let two or three ounces of fresh butter melt in a suitable stewpan, put in your bird, and let it heat gently over a slow fire—say fifteen to twenty minutes. Chop the liver along with a rasher of good bacon, two or three shalots, and a small seasoning of parsley and sweet herbs. Heat two ounces of bread crumbs in fresh butter over the fire until of a light yellow colour, then add the chopped liver, &c., and let it gently stew a short time over a slow fire. Boil an ounce of truffles, pared and sliced, and an ounce of chopped mushrooms in light Rhine wine (Laubenheimer will do). Now take the stewpan, with the bird in it, off the fire, drain the butter off, and add instead that with the stewed bread crumbs, liver, &c., also the wine with the truffles and

---

[*] It was in 1876, at the Salmon Hotel, in Kehl, near Strasburg.

mushrooms, half a pint of Laubenheimer or Niersteiner a large ladleful of good broth, the half of a lemon cut in slices (peel and pips removed), and a laurel leaf. Cover the stewpan close, set it again on the fire or hot plate, and let the bird stew slowly until it is nearly done. Then take the pan off the fire, and let the contents cool. Make your paste with fine flour and best fresh butter, and line a suitable pie dish with it. Lay in the peacock with the breast upward, covered with a thin rasher of fat bacon, cover as usual with paste, brush over with egg, and bake in a well heated oven forty to forty-five minutes. The colour ought to be bright yellow. Add to the sauce left in the stewpan, from which the bird has been transferred to the pie dish, a few ladlefuls of good broth and the juice of the other half of the lemon, and keep hot. Take the baked pie out of the oven, raise the top, and pour in the sauce. Stick the peacock's head on the top, and serve the pie hot.

I venture to hint that in stuffing TURKEY for roasting it may be found an improvement to substitute pork sausage meat for the suet as directed in cookery books, and to add to the stuffing a quarter of a pound of chopped sultana raisins. It may be found worth a trial.

Another hint. Instead of preparing apple sauce separately for ROAST GOOSE, take a suitable number of pippins or other sweet apples, pare them, remove

the core, and cut the apples in quarters. Stuff your
goose with them before putting it to the fire. They
will impart their flavour to the bird. A couple of
ounces of sultanas sprinkled among the apples will
improve the taste. Or the apples may be half roasted
in the oven before they are put into the goose.

In my earlier days I have often seen GOOSE DRIPPING
turned to excellent account by mixing it with an equal
quantity of pork dripping and twice the quantity of
beef dripping, all clarified and absolutely freed from
albuminous admixture; kneading this mass thoroughly,
and working half an ounce of fine salt to the pound
through it; washing slightly in cold water, and letting
it drain on a clean cloth. This is a better substitute
for butter than the abominations now so often palmed
upon the public. On one of my latest visits to
Hamburg I had some of this surrogate placed before
me, containing about one-eighth part of sound Holstein
butter. I cannot say I found this an improvement.
If the addition was intended to turn the mixture into
something like real butter, it certainly failed most
signally.

Being on the subject of that noble bird, the goose, I
take the opportunity of offering a few remarks on the
bird in general, its breeding and fattening, and on one
of its most interesting parts, physiologically and com-
mercially—the liver.

It may be cursorily observed here that we are
not very advanced yet in England in the breeding
and fattening of geese, that is to say in comparison
with certain parts of France, Holland, and Germany.
In the latter two countries the chief object of the
fattening process is the same as with us in England,
the production of solid, nutritious flesh, to wit, and
wholesome fat. But in certain parts of France,
more especially in Toulouse, and most of all in Strasburg, the object is to produce morbid enlargement
and fatty degeneration of the liver of the unhappy
bird.

Toulouse enjoys the great advantage of a very
fine, superior, race of geese, which, properly fed, will
attain to twice the weight of the common species. This
race is of broad and massive build, short-legged, and, as
a general rule, gray in plumage. A wide membraneous
bag or sack stretches from under the craw down to the
belly, which thus actually trails on the ground. Large
accumulations of fat find room within the folds of this
bag. As the fattening progresses the bird grows more
and more unwieldy, until at last it loses all power of
moving about.

This species of the genus goose is bred more
especially in the departments of the Garonne, Haute
Garonne, Tarn, Gers, and Ariège, where it forms well-
nigh the most important branch of rural industry.

Every farmer breeds larger or smaller flocks, from twenty upwards; some contenting themselves with getting a large number of goose eggs hatched by hens (I have lately heard that they have introduced the incubator in some parts) and selling the young broods, eight or ten days old, to people who make it their special business to prepare the birds for fattening by sending them to feed in the clover and stubble fields—the same as is done in Yorkshire—till they are fit for the final cramming process. Others work this business as a rural industry on a large scale, devoting to it extensive fields, turned into artificial meadows for the specific purpose of goose pasture.

In summer the birds are fattened chiefly for the fresh-meat market, in late autumn for salting.

The Alsatian goose is very inferior in size and weight to the Tolosan bird. Whilst the latter is often fattened up to from sixteen to twenty pounds weight, the Alsatian goose, with all the "superior" cramming, can hardly ever be forced up beyond twelve or, at the most, fourteen pounds.

The gray Dutch goose, which is imported into Alsatia, does not answer well for the great Strasburg *pâté de foie gras* industry, as the bird has a deal of Dutch obstinacy about it, and will not take kindly to cramming. The flesh, also, is rather inferior, as English housewives are apt to find when they buy the article in the market as imported, more particularly about Christmas.

There are two places in France and one in Germany where the famous goose-liver-pasty tureens are produced, to wit, Toulouse and Nérac, and Strasburg. The Nérac tureen, however, is a deception, being made of the liver of the musk duck.

Strasburg claims the honour of the first invention of this delicate but dyspeptic dish. A certain Mathieu, *chef* in the prince bishop of Strasburg, Cardinal Rohan's, household, was for a long time permitted to usurp the proud position of inventor of *pâté de foie gras.* But the real Simon Pure was a certain Close, the Marshal of Saxe's *chef,* who came to Strasburg in the train of his famous master, and took up his permanent abode there, marrying Mathieu's widow. It was he who started the goose liver tureen business in a small shop in the Meisengasse, where I was told it was still carried on to the present day.

In my frequent visits to and occasionally long stays at Strasburg, I have had ample opportunities of watching the goose-liver tureen industry from its first to its last stage, and I think a brief summary of my experience may not prove wholly uninteresting to the readers of this little book.

The fattening of geese for the tureen is carried on

very extensively in Strasburg, the handsome sum of one hundred thousand pounds sterling being realised annually by the sale of goose-liver tureens. The preliminary business is chiefly in the hands of women, and carried on almost exclusively in winter, the fatteners or "crammers" buying their birds late in autumn, either lean or half-fattened.

Maize soaked or parboiled in warm water slightly salted, occasionally alternating with balls of potato flour and barley meal, is the sole food with which the birds are crammed. Some crammers, however, deem it more economical to feed them on broad beans up to the last eight or ten days, when they also are put on a maize diet. With a very few exceptions, the unhappy birds are confined in narrow cages, barely wide enough to allow the poor prisoner to move a few inches backward and forward, but certainly not to turn round. There is a narrow opening in front, through which the bird may put its head to drink, a vessel of water being set before it—an indulgence which, I have been told, is not freely granted by *all* crammers, some of them fancying that unquenched thirst will make the liver swell! A lump of charcoal is generally placed with the water to ensure its purity. Great attention is paid to the cleanliness of the cage.

Some crammers will keep their birds closely caged up in cellars and dark places during the three or four weeks of their martyrdom, under the impression that deprivation of light also will do its share towards the coveted enlargement of the liver. A few, more humanely disposed, perhaps, or a little more sensible, will allow their fattening geese at least the enjoyment of the light of day and a little freedom of motion ; and I have had occasion, over and over again, to see that these trifling indulgences do not act adversely upon the development of the liver, as is generally urged by the cold-blooded advocates of the more cruel system. The geese are crammed twice or three times a day, according to the greater or lesser rapidity of digestion.

The poor bird is dragged forth, for the purpose, from its narrow cage by the feeder, who places it firmly between her knees, opens the beak with one hand, and crams the softened maize down the gullet with the other, generally simply with her finger. Less expert crammers use a funnel, with a smooth wood or ivory stick to expedite the descent of the food. When the feeder thinks the bird has had enough for one meal, she thrusts it back into its living tomb, leaving it to digest in helpless immobility its forced gorging, till its turn comes round again for another repetition in the same unnatural act in the same sad drama of suffering.

It takes from a fortnight to a month to cram a goose to the proper "sticking" or throat-cutting point.

In the last stage of the process it may be said literally to sweat fat through every pore of its body. The cellular tissue, the intestines, the blood, nay, even the evacuations, are absolutely loaded with fat. With regard to the latter most unsavoury item, I once, upon a visit to a crammer, accidentally saw the performance of a certain process of melting, which I was told, after, is quite common with Strasburg crammers, laudably bent upon utilising every part of the proceeds of their industry, but which gave me, with my foolish prejudice against unclean things, well-nigh inconvenient qualms of the stomach. I then and there registered a vow against goose fat, unless melted and rendered under my personal supervision, or procured from an unquestionably clean and decent source.

Now, under this cruelly unnatural treatment the liver of the goose swells to an enormous size, attaining a weight of one to two, and in some rare cases, even three pounds !

In the last stage of the fattening process the crammer has to be very watchful in the handling of her geese, as cases of apoplexy are by no means rare. An unlucky blow or a hard squeeze will often suffice to bring the unhappy bird's life to a premature close. I was once told by one of the best Strasburg crammers, that she was always carefully watching the eyes for threatening symptoms. If a goose is carried off by a fit, instead of

being properly despatched with the knife, the in-
dustrious crammer suffers a serious loss, as no pastrycook is likely to buy the discoloured liver for the
tureen, unless at a very low price for lining.

When the crammer judges the time has come for
poor fat goosey, the knife puts an end to its miserable
life. The quantity of Indian corn which it has been
made to gulp down during its gorging martyrdom,
averages about a quart a day. The dead bird is drawn,
but the liver is left intact inside, to let it acquire the
requisite firmness. To this end the bird is kept hanging for twenty-four hours in a cold and airy place, after
which the liver is taken out and the gall carefully
removed. When all is done properly, the liver shows
no scratch or other blemish; it looks a nice light
salmon or cream colour. It is now neatly wrapped
in wet muslin or fine linen cloth and taken to the
pastrycook.

The livers average in weight from one pound to two
pounds each. They are paid for by the pastrycook
according to size and quality, and to the actual condition of the market. A brisk demand makes the
livers look up, whilst a slack market depresses the price.
Taking the average of the five or six seasons that I
have known the trade, the prices have ranged from 3s.
to 3s. 6d. per pound for livers a little under a pound;
up to a pound and a half 3s. 9d. to 4s. 3d.; from a

pound and a half to two pounds, 4s. 6d. to 4s. 9d. ;
above two pounds, 5s. 6d. For exceptionally large
livers up to three pounds and a few ounces above,
I have seen paid as much as 7s. 6d. to 8s. 6d. per
pound.

The pastrycook divides the liver into two parts, at
the spot where the lobes join. He cuts out the part
that has been in immediate contact with the gall
bladder, which is generally marked by a yellowish tint,
and washes the cut surfaces with new milk. For a
tureen that will fetch from a guinea to twenty-five
shillings in the market, he takes three livers, one and a
quarter to one and a half pound each. This gives six
parts, of which he selects the four finest for the body of
the tureen. He pares about a pound of truffles, and
cuts three-fourths of them into thin and narrow strips,
about the length of a little finger. With these he
sticks the four half-livers all over. The remaining two
halves he cuts into very thin slices, which he pounds in
a mortar. He boils about two pounds of bacon for an
hour, lets them get cold, and cuts them up very fine.
He adds to the pounded liver one ounce and a half each
of shalots, mushrooms, and capers, the remainder of the
truffles chopped fine, four anchovies, boned, washed and
chopped, a teaspoonful of fine salt, and one of white
pepper and grated nutmeg, and the bacon. He pounds
and triturates the whole, and rubs the mass through

the tamis. He anoints the inside of the tureen all over
with fresh butter, and proceeds to fill it, putting in first
a layer of the stuffing or lining, then a half liver,
sprinkled with salt and white pepper; then another
layer of stuffing and another half liver, and so on a
third and a fourth, with a layer of the lining to finish
up. He now puts on the top a pound of fresh butter,
mixed with half an ounce of fine salt and white pepper,
spreading it out all over the top. He finishes up with
some slices of fat bacon, puts on the cover, pastes paper
all round, and bakes the *pâté* about two hours in a slow
oven. When done, he takes off the cover, and pours a
layer of hog's lard over the mass, to shield it from
the air.

Then the tureens are sent forth on their dyspeptic
mission to all parts of the world. I was once shown a
tureen in the Meisengasse with an exceptionally large
fine liver in it, weighing three pounds one ounce! This
went to General Fransecky, then commander of the
military district of Alsace-Lorraine, who paid £2 10s.
for it.

This liver gorging business is a wicked and cruel
industry at the best, whilst the product, though no
doubt most delicious to the palate of an epicure, cannot
possibly be wholesome. For my own part, I must confess that I prefer to it the excellent Brunswick liver
sausage, which, whilst very little less grateful to the

palate, is certainly a much sounder article of food, and has, at least, this great advantage in its favour, that it is not the product of an artificially created disease, entailing cruel suffering upon an unhappy race of most useful birds.

An excellent substitute for goose-liver tureen may be made with pig's liver, in the following way :—

Take a good-sized pig's liver, immerse it five or six minutes in hot water, chop it fine, and rub it through a tamis. Cut half a pound of bacon into very small cubes ; boil another half pound, and chop it : add the whole of the bacon to the liver, along with six soft-boiled and pulped onions, passed through a tamis, half a pound of pared and chopped truffles, a quarter pound chopped mushrooms, a teaspoon and a half fine salt, one white pepper, and one mixed spice ; add also a quartern of red Burgundy or port, and boil the whole to a thickish consistency. Pour it into a suitable mould lined with bacon, and bake it from one and a half to two hours in a moderately heated oven. When baked put weights on, which will cause a good deal of fat to gather on the top. This fat must not be removed; but should any gravy make its appearance, it may be poured off with proper care. I have seen this substitute more than once on breakfast tables in London and other parts, where it passed unsuspected for the genuine article.

In terminating this half-digression, anent the
dyspeptic offspring of Master Close's culinary genius,
I crave permission to tell a little apologue which I
read many years ago in a collection of German poems.

The Prince of Midnight—Death—once upon a time
summoned the two houses of his Black Parliament, that
he might appoint a new prime minister, the then holder of
the office—Yellow Jack, if I remember rightly—wishing
to retire. Numerous candidates presented themselves,
among others the Plague, who proudly referred in proof
of her superior qualifications to the prayer in the
Litany. This seemed conclusive, and the dread king
was on the point of bestowing the coveted high office
upon the distinguished claimant, when a new candidate
rose, who boasted that he was the largest purveyor to
the universal shambles. " Who are you, then ?" queried
the puzzled king, who could not remember having ever
seen him before. "A cook, sire," was the reply, given
with the proud emphasis of conscious merit. I have a
notion he was a pastrycook from Strasburg, and his
name was Close.

The capercailzie, or cock of the wood, also known as
wood grouse and mountain cock (*Tetrao urogallus*),
ought to rank high in the list of game fowl. But I am
afraid it is not appreciated in England. In my long
experience I have but rarely seen it on an English
table, and, I am sorry to add, not always properly done.

My friend Draper, at whose hospitable board I have repeatedly had the good fortune to eat it done to perfection, writes to me upon the interesting subject as follows :—

"This is our way of treating our friend capercailzie, according to his deserts: We simply roast him, and serve with pickled pork, the 'belly part' being the best; also with bread sauce. As a domestic meal this noble bird is but little used in England, in consequence of popular ignorance of his qualities. In carving, cut slices of the breast only, leaving the limbs for future service. The external muscles will be found of a rich game brown, and the internal as white and delicate as the flesh of chicken. The next day hash the legs and wings with good stock, and a dash of such piquant sauce as may be desired. Pickled walnut liquor, sparingly used, will be found very good."

It is a condition precedent, however, that the bird should be young. Older birds are apt to prove tough customers. To make them more amenable to mastication, sprinkle the properly drawn and cleansed bird inside and out with ground pepper, allspice, ginger, and wood charcoal; sew it up in canvas, bury in the ground some three to four feet deep, and leave it there a fortnight. Even this will but rarely answer the purpose, however, and hardly ever with very old birds. This may be the reason in part why the cock of the wood is

I

so little patronised; the first trial—which was to prove
the fact—having unluckily been made with an irre-
mediably tough bird. Still, even old capercailzies may,
after a fortnight's burial, be turned to good account for
ragouts and fricassees.

The subjoined recipe, taken from the German, combines the processes of stewing and roasting in the oven.
I have had occasion to try it, and I can fairly recommend it.

Take a young capercailzie, let it hang a few days in
a cool and airy place, then have it properly drawn and
cleaned. Chop half a pound of veal cutlet and half a
pound of raw ham, with a fair share of fat to it, very
fine; add six ounces of grated bread, a drachm of pounded
cloves, half a teacupful of thick sweet cream, and a
teaspoonful of salt; stir in the yolk of three eggs, with
the well-beaten whites, and mix thoroughly. Some add
three or four shalots, a few sprigs of lemon thyme, and
half an ounce each of mushrooms and truffles—all finely
chopped. Addition of four ounces each of rump steak
and pork, finely chopped, the grated peel of a lemon,
with the juice, is also recommended. I feel much inclined, from my own experience, to look upon these
additions as improvements.

Put in the stuffing, and cover the bird's breast with
thin slices of fat bacon. Lay slices of bacon at the
bottom of a suitable pan, with a quarter of a pound of

butter; add boiling water, and put the bird in breast upwards. Cover the pan close, and let the bird stew at a gentle but continuous boil until the flesh is nearly tender. Pour off the gravy into a basin, and put another quarter of a pound of butter in the pan; take the cover off, and let your bird roast in a hot oven until it is nicely yellow, basting it assiduously all the time, and adding the gravy in the basin gradually, along with half a cupful of thick, sweet cream—stir in two teaspoonfuls of fine flour, and add just enough cold water to make a thickish sauce. Serve on a very hot dish, garnished round the rim with thin slices of bacon.

A capercailzie pie is another very dainty dish. Take a young bird, let it hang three or four days, take out all the bones, and cut up the flesh into small pieces; fry these very lightly in butter, then lay them a few hours in vinegar, with pepper, nutmeg, and two or three small onions or shalots. Meanwhile chop six ounces to half a pound each of veal, beef, and fresh pork, very fine; add six ounces of bread crumbs, and a quarter of an ounce of grated nutmeg and pounded cloves, with the yolks of three hard-boiled eggs finely chopped; stir in a raw yolk, and mix thoroughly. Lay a few lumps of butter and slices of fat bacon at the bottom of a pie mould, then fill the latter with the flesh of the bird and the chopped meat, &c., in alternate layers. Put

slices of lemon on the top, sprinkle salt over, and pour
in half a bottle of wine. Then cover the mould close,
and keep it four or five hours on a gentle fire. If you
find it getting over-dry, you may add another quartern
of wine or so. When well done, remove the lemon, and
thicken the gravy with the yolk of an egg or two, and
serve the pie cold.

Just a hint or two anent hares. Never buy a hare
with the spine smashed by shot. Young hares are the
best for roasting. Old animals answer better for soup
and rágout. Hares should always be kept hanging—
young animals four to six, old ones eight to ten days,
always supposing, of course, you get them quite fresh
from the poulterer. Sudden changes of temperature
from cold to comparatively warm will have to be taken
into account. Some recommend to skin, draw, and
cleanse the animal after a few days' hanging, then rub
it all over inside and out with pounded wood charcoal
and ground ginger, and let it hang for several days
longer in an airy place. An old hare may be fitted for
roasting by laying it for three or four days in buttermilk, with frequent turning. This makes the flesh
much more tender. A young hare should be laid for
twenty-four hours in new milk, taking care to ladle the
milk from time to time over it, to keep all parts
as uniformly as practicable in contact with the milk.
Well-seasoned veal stuffing is an improvement. I always

add an equal quantity of sausage meat to it. Lard your hare well in two double rows along the spine on both sides. Baste the roasting hare assiduously with plenty of good butter. Towards the end, when the hare is roasted to a nice light yellow, pour a cupful or two of thick, sweet cream over it. The roast so prepared will be found truly delicious and most succulent.

CHAPTER II.

FISH is an excellent article of food, and may well claim
to figure in every dietary. In its well nigh infinite
variety, prepared by every conceivable process of cooking, it supplies man with an almost inexhaustible source
of tasty and wholesome dishes. However, it is inferior
in nutritive value to flesh food, as it contains a larger
proportion of water. So, though a most valuable
auxiliary, it makes but an indifferent principal food,
and people who have to subsist entirely and exclusively
upon it are ill fed and worse nourished ; though this—
perhaps even as it stands somewhat sweeping remark—
may certainly be taken to apply to a limited degree
only to the king of the red bloods—the salmon. As
fish contains a larger proportion of phosphorus than
flesh foods, it is especially advantageous in the dietary
of brain workers, and those oppressed with care and
anxiety.

All fresh water and unsalted fish should be cooked

fresh: they are always best in every way if prepared
for the table on the day they are caught, although some
of them *may* be kept till next day or even the day
after, particularly in cold weather. Some fish, such as
the trout, for instance, will keep only a few hours.
From a strangely mistaken analogy some people seem
to entertain a dim notion that keeping fish a day or
two improves its flavour. I do not wish to appear
dogmatic, but I *cannot* refrain from expressing my
absolute and uncompromising dissent from that notion.
The liver and also the soft roe of certain fish taken in
rivers and ponds—the red gurnet, the carp, &c.—are
delicate morsels, which keeping over night is almost
sure to spoil. The livers of sea fish are utterly un-
palatable, having a strong flavour of train oil.

Stale fish ought to be scrupulously avoided. To say the
very least of it, it is nasty, and certainly often unwholesome. It is never advisable, therefore, to buy fish in the
streets unless it have about it all the signs of freshness
generally recognised as indispensable—lively red gills,
bright eyes, and general stiffness. Fish is also always
the better for being killed promptly after being taken
out of its element, instead of being let die a lingering
death, as is but too often done, be it from sheer ignorance or from callous indifference to the suffering of
the animal.

Fish is cooked by boiling, stewing, baking, broiling,

or frying. The first of these processes is by no means the most tasty way of preparing fish for the table, nor is it economical, as a notable portion of the nutritive juices escapes into the water. Broiling, where applicable, is a much better way, the fish being more tasty, and no loss of substance incurred.

Baking, stewing, and frying are also superior ways of preparing fish for the table.

"Salting," says Mr. Tegetmeier, " though often necessary to preserve fish when caught in large quantities, is not a desirable mode of preparing white fish. It extracts a very large proportion of the nourishment and hardens the fibrin; and if the salt has to be extracted by soaking in water before cooking, as in the case of salt cod, very little nourishment remains. The fat of the oily fish, as herring, &c., is not removed by salting; hence they are very valuable as food when preserved in this manner."

Fresh water fish has occasionally a musty smell and taste, which a few hours' immersion in a strong solution of salt in water will remove.

Fish is most commonly cooked in the mass, but occasionally it is cut in slices. This operation is called crimping.

Fresh water fish, unless of large size, is generally put into boiling water, and removed from the fire after a short time. Large fresh water and sea fish is, as a rule, put into cold water, set to boil very gently, and removed from the fire when fully boiling. Crimp fish is put into boiling water. It is recommended by some to check the boiling by the addition of cold water. Without disparaging this proceeding, I must say, I prefer reducing the temperature by removing the fish kettle, &c., to a more moderately heated part of the hot plate.

Fish that is being cooked just after being caught and killed had always better be put into cold water, or moderately warm water first, as rapid boiling tends to break the outside before the inside part is done.

"Sturgeon," writes my friend, Draper, "is another unjustly neglected food in England. There are two ways to prepare it for the table that may be equally commended. If you have a piece of moderate weight, say three to four pounds, stuff it as veal, and roast in the usual way; serve with lemon. The other way is to divide the fish into cutlets, dip them in batter, and fry in good salad oil—as fish should always be fried."

I quite agree with Mr. Draper in his recommendation of good salad oil for frying fish—of course the oil must be olive oil and sweet—the least taint of rancidity unfits it for this particular use, at least. In France and in Germany rape seed oil is used rather largely, both for frying and for salads. In Germany, they prepare a special fat for frying, by melting together equal parts of hog's lard and beef suet, and stirring in a third equal part of rape seed oil, so that the frying mixture consists of equal parts of rape-seed oil, lard and suet. Among other substitutes, poppy oil is also largely used, especially to adulterate olive oil with. If quite sweet no great harm is done. The adulteration may easily be detected, as olive oil congeals in the cold, whilst poppy oil remains limpid. Rancid oils of whatever kind are objectionable, but the most objectionable of all is the oil—olive or other— which has been used for successive days or weeks to fry fish in.

Some fifty years ago, I was hospitably entertained on several occasions by some Spanish officers, stationed on the Mediterranean coast, near Algiers. Among other dishes, they placed before me a delicious mess of small fish and sliced apples fried in alternate layers, with salt and brown sugar sprinkled between. After a time, however, their oil got rancid and day by day fishier, as my friends persisted in using it over and over again. The result was, that I gave their quarters the widest possible berth, and that the merest thought of fish and apples was nauseating to me.

In Germany they practise a very simple and equally effective way to improve rape seed oil. The oil, in a pretty large pot, is heated to boiling. A crust of black bread moistened with water is then thrown in, and the

pot kept on the fire ten minutes longer. It is then
removed to the sink, and a few drops of cold water are
sprinkled on it. This causes a slight bubbling on the surface and a strong smell. The same operation is repeated
twice or thrice, until no further bubbling is observed.
When quite cold, the oil is filled into suitable bottles
or flasks, closed with stoppers or corks, and kept for use
in a cool place. Another even more simple way is to
throw a few potatoes cut in thin slices into the oil in the
pot, which is set on a slow fire or, better, on the hot plate,
and let them fry a light brown, which generally takes
fifteen to twenty minutes ; then throw in a few grains
of salt; if no more scum rises, the oil may be considered
fit for use.

With Mr. Draper's remark about the unjust neglect
of sturgeon in England I most fully concur. This
neglect is the offspring of ignorance and prejudice,
fostered and fed by more than one of those influential
writers "on all things and a great many other things
besides," who would mould and fashion public notions
of most matters, social and political, upon their own
preconceptions, occasionally formed in haste and without
mature consideration.

Once upon a time I had a rather warm discussion
with a very dear friend, now no more, upon the subject
of Voltaire's 'Philosophical Dictionary,' which said
friend utterly and uncompromisingly condemned as

blasphemous, obscene, infamous, lying, ignorant, and a full string of such-like epithets. I humbly ventured to dissent, suggesting that he had, most likely, only read an article here and there, and urging him to give the book and its author a fairer trial. " Read an article here and there!" my friend shouted, indignantly; "why, sir, I thought you knew me better than to imagine I ever could or would read one word of such pestilential writings."

Well, somewhat similarly, another friend, a late distinguished writer, who would occasionally stray into the domain of cookery, suddenly evinced a dislike to the poor sturgeon—I thought at first it must have been after a surfeit of *caviare*—but his uncompromising repudiation of every and any part of the assailed fish undeceived me. He strove to the utmost of his power and gifts to talk and write the unhappy fish down, as being train-oily, hard, nasty-flavoured, indigestible, &c., &c. "Have you ever eaten nicely fried sturgeon cutlets, or sturgeon stew?" I ventured to ask my irate friend. "Eaten sturgeon stew or cutlet!" he cried with angry amazement. "Goodness gracious! I would never let any preparation of that nasty thing come near my mouth. I would as lief eat porbeagles, Canterbury gurnet, and dog fish. My poor mother hated the very sight and smell of it." —which of course was a logical and convincing argument. Now a sturgeon stew is really an excellent dish

which may be prepared after several approved recipes—
I can recommend the following way. Cut about five
pounds of the middle part of a good sound sturgeon in
slices about an inch thick. Fry these just to incipient
light yellowness in a mixture of equal parts of good
butter and sweet olive oil. Take the cutlets out and
put them in a stew pan with veal broth flavoured with
two teaspoonfuls of Liebig's Extract of Meat, a little salt,
pepper, cloves, and mace. Add four shalots, two ounces
of white mushrooms, and two of parsley, a few sprigs of
lemon thyme, a bunch of savoury, sage, and sweet marjoram, all finely chopped; set the stew pan on a gentle
fire or a hot plate, and let the cutlets stew slowly until
they are quite tender. Fry a thin-sliced onion in the
butter and oil in which the cutlets have been fried, stir
in a spoonful of flour to browning, add a spoonful of
ketchup, one of Worcester sauce, the juice of half a
lemon, and a quartern of Hock or Chablis. Take the
cutlets out of the gravy, and set them in a suitable dish
on the hot plate. Pour the contents of the frying pan
into the stew pan with the gravy in which the cutlets
have been stewed. Let the whole boil up, strain, and
pour over the cutlets in the dish.

For BOILING, sturgeon should be put in cold water,
without salt, but with a handful of stinging nettles—
which serve to extract the train oil and promote the
softening of the fish. It is only after the sturgeon is

tender that salt should be added, and the fish left some time after in the gravy to take up the salt.

The CONGER EEL also may be said to be under a species of ban in England, at least with most people, although it is much esteemed in the form of soup, more particularly in the Channel Islands. The recipe of conger eel soup may be found in nearly every cookery book, perhaps also, conger eel pie; but baked, fried and stewed conger may be looked for in vain in Archimagi- rical manuals. Yet the fish is really excellent food in nearly every form of preparation—even as an adjunct to turtle soup, as an eminent Professor has recently stated, thereby bringing down on his devoted head the indignant denial and the angry denunciations of some of the most distinguished purveyors of that expensive luxury. I am perfectly convinced that these protesting gentlemen never dream of using conger as an ingredient in their turtle; but I think I may aver that it is used occasionally by some of the less scrupulous of the craft. I can, from my personal experience, affirm that in times of yore, I have been applied to more than once by professional caterers to assist them in "lengthening" turtle soup with conger. I will even go farther; I truly believe that conger, judiciously used, is an improvement on turtle rather than otherwise, especially where the soup is made with *small* turtles, as I have often known to be the case in England. Moreover, among the truly bewildering variety of ingredients required to make up genuine turtle soup, a conger may not be quite so incongruous as it looks at the outside.

Conger is certainly very inferior to river eel, particularly to the eel caught in Irish rivers. It contains a much larger proportion of water (five to four, I think); but it contains also much less fat (something like five to twenty-four), which to me seems rather an advantage than otherwise.

I know the conger is largely eaten by the poorer classes in Ireland. My personal experience here on the south eastern coast leads me to believe that even the poor feel disposed to slight it as a food, except in the form of soup, perhaps. I have actually seen Ramsgate fishermen throw it back into the water, or generously bestow it gratis upon the first suitor for it. No fishmonger of any pretention in Ramsgate will sell it; and I have often bought it in King Street at the modest figure of twopence a pound, at the very time when it was selling in London (for soup) at fourpence halfpenny a pound.

No doubt conger requires some preparation to fit it for the several processes of cooking. This preparation, however, is very simple. Cut your conger, as fresh as ever you can get it, into pieces, rub these over with ground pepper and cloves, and place them in a deep dish, with a handful or two of stinging-nettles thrown among

them. Mix a pint of best Orleans vinegar with a
pint of water, and dissolve three half ounces of salt in the
mixture. Pour this brine over the conger in the dish,
and let it stand twenty-four hours, turning it over
frequently, to ensure equal contact of every part with
the liquid. Then wash the eel well, keep it an hour or
so in cold water, wipe every piece quite dry, and bake,
fry, or stew as directed in cookery books. The following
way of preparing a truly savory conger eel stew has been
often tried with perfect success. Dredge the conger pieces
with flour, and fry them a light brown in butter or
sweet olive oil (I prefer the latter). Lay a few thin
slices of fat bacon at the bottom of a suitable stew-pan.
Take four or five shalots, four ounces of white mushrooms, two ounces of parsley, and a bunch of sweet
herbs, tarragon, and fennel, and chop very fine ; add the
peel of a lemon grated, a teaspoonful of salt, and an
ounce of ground black pepper, cloves, and Jamaica
pepper, and mix thoroughly. Strew a portion of the
mixture over the bacon at the bottom, lay some pieces
of the conger on this, then another sprinkle of seasoning, and so on. Add to a quart of your stock a teaspoonful of Liebig's Extract, a tablespoonful of Worcester
sauce, one of ketchup, and the juice of half a lemon.
Pour over the conger in the pan. The liquid should
nearly cover the fish. So more has to be added where
this is not the case. Cover the pan close, and let it

stew very gently on the hot-plate until the flesh comes easily off the bones. Add a small teacupful of sherry to the gravy, and thicken with a little flour.

HERRING is one of the most valuable articles of food. " Under ordinary circumstances," says Dr. Smith, " fresh herring offers the largest amount of nutriment for a given sum of money of any kind of animal food. A fresh herring weighing four and a half ounces, and costing one halfpenny,* contains two hundred and forty grains of carbon and thirty-six grains of nitrogen ; and a dried herring weighing three ounces, and costing three farthings, contains two hundred and sixty-nine grains of carbon and forty-one grains of nitrogen."

Fresh herring is a most perishable commodity, unfortunately ; so that its occasional exceptional cheapness is not always the boon it might be ; but it may be kept for a time by pickling, or marinading, it, in the following way : Scrape, clean, wash and dry your herrings, anoint them all over with sweet oil, sprinkle them with salt and ground black and Jamaica pepper, and grill them on both sides (brownish) on the gridiron. Place a layer of laurel leaves, thyme, lemon thyme, fennel, tarragon, a few cloves and cuttings of lemon peel at the bottom of an earthen pan or stone jar. Put a layer of your grilled herrings on this, then again a layer of

---

* I have bought them in places on the English sea coast over and over again forty and even more for one shilling.

seasoning, and so on. Boil salt in vinegar (three half-
ounces to the quart), let the sour brine cool, and pour it
over the fish in the pot or jar. Tie oiled parchment
paper over the pot or jar, and keep it in a cool place.

Salt herrings, especially Dutch, are marinaded best as
follows : Scrape, clean, and wash your herrings, setting
the roes aside. Put the herrings so prepared two days
in milk ; or, if this seems to come too expensive, simply
in water. But milk is best. You may cut off the heads
and tails, but there is no absolute need. To one dozen
of herrings take a nutmeg grated, one ounce of white
mustard seeds, and twelve white peppercorns, with a
dozen cloves, all pounded in a mortar, and eight shalots,
very finely chopped. Put an equal portion of the mixture
with each herring. Cut a large Spanish onion or two into
very thin slices, do the same with two fine lemons, taking
care to remove the peel and the pips. Cut two good-
sized salt-pickled cucumbers—so-called " saure Gurken,"
which may be got at any German provision shop—and
about half-a-dozen pickled gherkins in pieces. Chop
two ounces of capers fine with a bunch of sweet herbs
and tarragon, and add a few laurel leaves. Mix all
these ingredients, and put them with the herrings in
alternate layers in a stone jar. Work up the roes of
the herrings (soft roes should always as far as practicable be selected in preference) with good French vinegar
into a thickish sauce, which pour over the herrings

&c., in the jar; tie over with oiled parchment paper, and keep in a cool place. In eight to ten days the herrings are ready for eating.

Many years ago poor dear Charles Sala showed me how to cook a bloater to perfection by a new system, professedly invented by him, which I may say I found excellent. Only it has the trifling drawback of being a trifle expensive. It is easy to do : You take a large soup plate and pour a quartern of the best whisky into it; you then lay two fine bloaters on the plate, set fire to the spirit, and turn the bloaters over and over again in the burning whisky. When the spirit is consumed, the herrings are done to perfection. A good dish, but *not* economical, at least not in the United Kingdom, where the duty on spirits fluctuates between ten and twelve shillings a gallon.

Another dear friend of mine, who I am happy to say is still to the fore, Horwitz, the famous chess-player and artist, is equally great in fish cooking. I learnt much from him on that special line of the art, more particularly the proper way of preparing carp *à le polonaise*, *i.e.*, with beer sauce, as follows :—

Clean and wash your carps (fresh killed, if practicable), scale and split them, and cut them in pieces, reserving the blood in a wineglassful of fresh vinegar. To three or four pounds weight of carp take four carrots, half a turnip, two or three parsley roots, a quarter of a celery root ; slice the carrots, &c., add a few cloves, peppercorns, bits of ginger, a bunch of savory, thyme, sweet marjoram, and tarragon, and two laurel leaves or three. Boil all these ingredients in a stew-pan about fifteen to twenty minutes in a quart of unhopped beer, such as Drogheda ale, for instance, or Edinburgh ale— *bitter* beer will not do.* We used sweet Edinburgh ale for our Polish sauce. After fifteen to twenty minutes boiling lay in the carp, sprinkle a teaspoonful of fine salt over it—according to requirement—add half a lemon in slices, removing the peel and the pips, three or four finely chopped shalots fried a light yellow, a quarter of a pound of butter, and the vinegar with the blood ; cover the pan close, and let it boil another fifteen minutes or so, when the fish will be well done. Take the fish out of the pan, and lay it in a dish on the hot-plate. Thicken the sauce with crumbled gingerbread, add a quartern of port wine, rub through a tamis, and pour one half over the fish, the other half into a sauce-boat. In Germany they mix the beer with an equal quantity of water, which Horwitz considered a work of supererogation.†

---

* I have found stout or porter do very well instead of sweet ale.

† No reflection on the brewer. I remember how once upon a time I roused the fiery indignation of a respectable publican by jocularly telling him that there was a deal of water in his beer, and how hard I found it to make him understand at last that beer could not possibly be brewed without a deal of water.

SHELLFISH, or CRUSTACEANS, may be dismissed briefly. The LOBSTER and the CRAYFISH are dearer than the CRAB, and are held to be more delicate in flavour. They are all three very pleasant food, but rather indigestible, as Quilp sagely remarks. The crab is the least indigestible of the three, and all things considered, may be said to be preferable as food to the lobster and the crayfish, with their tougher muscular structures. They contain little oil, and would be rather dry eating but for the generally adopted way of preparing them, to wit, with oil, vinegar and condiments, in the form of salad.

The first, or killing, stage of the process of preparing lobsters, &c. for eating cannot but be most harrowing to the feelings of the humane; the unfortunate animals are thrown alive into boiling water, which *must* be horribly painful to them. They are said to shriek with pain in dying. This is, of course, a trope, as the sufferers lack the organs indispensable for crying or shrieking. The harrowing cry would seem to arise simply from the spasmodic friction of the claws and shells. It is said that if the lobster, &c., is thrown into the bubbling water head foremost death is instantaneous. This should, therefore, always be scrupulously attended to, under any circumstances, even though the hot steam may prove troublesome and even somewhat hurtful to the hands dropping the lobster into the boiling fluid. A pound of salt has to be added per gallon of water, and the fluid ought to be on the bubbling boil when the shellfish is thrown in. It is advisable to close the lobster's vent with a wooden peg, or else too much water may get in. When the shellfish is thrown in, a red hot poker should be simultaneously plunged into the water, to ensure its being kept on the full boil. The same operation should be repeated after a few minutes. The boiling takes from one-half to one hour, according to size. When done, take the lobster from the hot water with the tongs and lay it on a cloth or a sheet of blotting paper to drain. Wipe it clean, and rub it over with a rind of bacon or a little butter.

Although death by boiling water must be acutely painful even to shellfish, whatever comfortable philosophers may think or say of the matter, the unhappy animal is after all not quite so badly treated by us as it was by our ancestors some three hundred years ago, when it was roasted alive in its shell in an oven or in a pan ; or as it is treated now-a-days in Italy, where they cut the live crawfish in two, to stew it in white wine, &c.

Lobster salad is made much more easily digestible, I think, by mixing it with lettuce or endive and other green stuff. For my way of preparing this delicacy I refer the reader to the chapter on Salads.

A lobster and crab figure among the ingredients in

Pepperpot, a favourite dish with epicures, which I not unfrequently have had occasion to prepare. The following is my recipe:—Stew six pounds of gravy beef in two gallons of water, with four ounces each of celery and parsley, three ounces of shalots and four of small white mushrooms (buttons), all chopped very fine, a bunch of tarragon, chervil, savory, sweet marjoram and lemon thyme. Let it simmer until the liquid is reduced to five quarts. Skim and let the skimmed fluid cool; take the fat off and pour the liquor into a stew-pan. Mince the flesh of a small lobster, a middling-sized crab, and a tin of Rock Bay lobster (which is an excellent article, nearly as good as fresh lobster, and much cheaper) Cut twelve ounces of cold bacon into small pieces, mince half-a-pound of broiled *lean* pork chops, a quarter of a pound of broiled veal cutlets. Beat two or three ounces of new-made unsalted butter to cream; stir in two yolks, add the rind of a lemon grated, an ounce of salt, and a quarter of an ounce of nutmeg grated; add also two ounces and a half of bread soaked in milk and squeezed as dry as practicable. Mix all these ingredients thoroughly, and work the white of an egg well beaten through the mass, which make into small meat-balls. Boil three-quarters of a peck of spinach, and rub through a colander. Heat the liquor in the stew-pan, and put in the whole of the above ingredients (except the minced meat of the lobster and crab), together with a pound of asparagus tops, the juice of a lemon, a table-spoonful of ketchup, and salt and cayenne to taste. Stew for about half-an-hour, with constant stirring. Just a few minutes before the stew is taken off the fire, add the minced meat of the lobster and crab, as this should never be boiled twice over, which would only make it more indigestible. Some add also a boiled fowl, but I think there is no need of this. I have a notion the dish is quite complex enough as it stands.

CHAPTER III.

MOLLUSCS AND TURTLE.

MOLLUSCS are represented chiefly by the oyster. The
mussel, whelk, cockle, limpet, periwinkle and scallop
also belong to the order. They are are not very
nutritious as food. They are soft, and most easily
masticated and digested.

Mussels, whelks, cockles, limpets, periwinkles, and
scallops are abundant on our shores, and afford cheap
food for the poorer classes. Mussels, if the beard has
not been properly cleaned away from them, are apt to
produce painful irritation of the skin, attended by febrile
symptoms.

A dose of quinine and compresses moistened with
sedative water applied to the rash will generally speedily
remove the inconvenience. Sedative water may easily
be made. Take an ounce of spirit of hartshorn, half-
an ounce of camphorated spirit of wine, and two ounces
of bay salt or of common salt. Dissolve the salt in a

quart of water; decant, and add the hartshorn and camphor to the decanted fluid, and bottle. Shake frequently. In the course of a month or so you will have a clear solution. For use, dilute part of the fluid with two or three parts of water, and moisten the lint or compress with the diluted liquid. This *en passant*.

Oysters, more especially the *Ostrea edulis*, have now become a delicacy, altogether out of the reach of the humbler classes. Nay, even the somewhat better-to-do cannot well afford to indulge in natives, least of all in Whitstables, but have to content themselves with the Virginian, the Blue-point, the Portuguese, the Dutch, and the French, as imported.

I have known the time when I have feasted in Hamburg on first-rate oysters at the moderate figure of 3*d.* a dozen; and I remember well those glorious old days, nigh half a century ago now, when authors, actors, and artists used to discuss, for tenpence or a shilling, their dozen of natives, including bread and butter and a glass of stout, at "Rule's," in Maiden Lane, and at "Godwin's," in the Strand, where the illustrious Charlotte dispensed molluscs and crustaceans alike at equally moderate charges. *Tempi passati.* In those days the London oyster season opened on the 5th of August and closed in May. At present it lasts from the 1st January to the 31st December. Many of our oyster-beds, from which we used to draw our best supplies, have been impoverished, and some even altogether destroyed; and it will take many a long year before we can reasonably hope to restore our supplies. As to the old prices ever ruling again in the oyster market, it would be over sanguine to expect it. Salmon was at one time the poor man's food: is it at all likely that it ever will be so again?

The oyster is mostly eaten uncooked, with lemon or vinegar, and pepper or cayenne. It is also made into patties, stews, scallops and sauces, &c. It should be borne in mind, however, that all processes of cooking tend to harden the oyster. Many, many long years ago, when a boy, I was fond of *Huîtres farcies*, or stuffed oysters, a Russian delicacy, prepared by opening a dozen oysters in the deep shells, bearding them, rinsing them in their own liquid, then putting in each a mince of basil, thyme, savory, parsley, shalot, two or three capers, a small mushroom, all finely chopped, grated lemon-peel, the size of a small nut of butter, a few grains of cayenne, a little roast veal, finely minced, and some pounded biscuit (unsweetened), moistened with half a dozen drops of lemon-juice and twice as much Madeira wine—(Marsala will do equally well; so will Hock or Chablis)—covering them with their shell, and baking them in a hot oven, in a pan with concave cover filled with live charcoal. Blue points, Portuguese, French, and Dutch oysters will do for this dish.

BAKED OYSTERS in the German fashion are prepared
in a very simple way:—Open your oysters—blue points
or others of the less expensive kind—beard them, and
remove them from the shell. Roll them in a batter of
egg, strongly seasoned with mace, then in pounded
biscuit (not sweet), and let them just stiffen in boiling
butter in a clean pan. Do not carry the process further,
or your oyster will be hard.

A good OYSTER SAUCE may be made as follows :—
Open two or three dozen of oysters, of the less expensive
sort, according to the number of persons at table, reckoning three to four oysters per head ; beard them, and
let the beards boil in good broth, with a little coarsely-
pounded white pepper and a laurel leaf in it, and pass
through a tamis. Stir a tablespoonful of flour in a few
ounces of boiling butter until the mass is just on the
point of rising. Then stir in the tamined broth, with half
a nutmeg grated, a glass of white wine, the juice of a
lemon, and the yolk of an egg or two. Finally, lay in
the oysters and their liquor, and add salt if needed. It
would not do to let the oysters boil with the other
ingredients, as it would simply harden them.

The large fine TURTLE and the REAL TURTLE SOUP I
dare not touch, nor touch upon. Why, even the great
Carême, the King of *Chefs* in his own time, and likely
to be considered so for ages to come, speaks of this
wondrous compound with something like awe. The

recipe, he says, is the most lengthened in its details of any ever excogitated in culinary brains. The composition of the seasoning claims an able hand and a strong memory; the palate of the *chef* called upon to perform the feat of preparing it requires the acutest sensitiveness, as it should be able to detect any ingredient that may predominate, however slightly.

The CONGER TURTLE of my own personal experience, alluded to in the chapter on Fish, is after all only an imitation of the real article, although small turtles enter into its composition; and I have known hundreds of people who never knew the difference.

Dr. Smith, in his great work on Foods, makes some most pertinent and true remarks (in my humble opinion) anent turtle, which, he says, "though so costly and favourite a food here, is neither scarce nor good in the tropical regions where it is produced. The number of these creatures lying on the sandy banks when depositing their eggs, or floating in the shallow bay, is almost infinite, so that they might be the sole animal food of the inhabitants of those regions; but neither the people who live among them, nor sailors who remain there temporarily, can continue to eat them."

Dr. Smith then has the following quotation from Bates' "Naturalist on the River Amazon:"—

" The abundance of turtles, or rather the facility with which they can be found and caught, varies with the annual subsidence of the water. When the river falls less than the average, they are scarce; when more, they can be caught in plenty, as the bays and the shallow lagoons in the forests have then only a small depth of water. The flesh is very tender, palatable, and wholesome; but it is very cloying; every one ends sooner or later by becoming thoroughly surfeited. I became so sick of turtle in the course of two years that I could not bear the smell of it, even when there was nothing else to to be had, and I was suffering actual hunger."

"With such testimony," continues Dr. Smith, "how may we explain the favour with which turtle soup has always been received by civilised nations, and the price asked and paid for it? Simply by the mode of preparation for the table. The flesh is never served separately, but is made into soup with a great variety of condiments, expensive wines, like Madeira, and other agreeable adjuncts, and with high culinary skill. The soup so prepared is doubtless luscious and rich, if not easily digestible; but if, instead of being rare and costly, it were a common and cheap diet, as it might be on tropical coasts, the appetite would soon reject it, and disease rather than health would follow its use. It must also be added that, as at present consumed, it is accompanied by costly viands and wines, which lend a gourmand's charms to the entertainment."

I append to this part a few remarks anent three

comestibles which, though seemingly classed together
here rather incongruously, have this feature in common,
that they are, though for different reasons, not generally
used for food—TRIPE, to wit, SNAILS, and the hind-legs
of the FROG.

TRIPE is easily masticated and digested, and, with
1705 grains of carbon and 143 grains of nitrogen in each
pound, might be classed with the more nutritious ali-
mentary substances, but that its nitrogenous constituents
are rather gelatinous than albuminous, which detracts
from their nutritive value, and that the article is over-
easily digested, thus failing to satisfy the stomach,
which soon craves for another supply of food. The
flavour also is not very pronounced; and even the sick,
for whose eating it would seem to be specially adapted,
have no great liking for it generally. Therefore,
except among the poor, it is rather an exceptional dish,
although it may be made very tasty by stewing it in
milk, and serving it with a rich white onion sauce. In
D'Olier Street, Dublin there is a restaurant where they
dispense, on Wednesdays and Fridays, savory half-crown
dinners of tripe and cowheel, which, it would appear,
are in brisk demand. However, I have a notion the
price may have something to do with this. I remember,
about half a century ago, when I was living at Lyons, a
young Marseillais was benevolently started in business
by a fellow townsman of his, who happened to be an

intimate friend of mine, and a most practical man of the
vastest capacity.

The young man knew how to prepare snails for
eating in a variety of ways. So Peyrade—the name of
his generous patron—directed the words "Spécialite
d'Escargots" to be painted on the signboard over his
door. The ingenuous youth proposed to supply his
delicacies at thirty sous (1s. 3d.) a dish; but his more
experienced patron coolly put them at five francs a dish.
I at first doubted the wisdom of this; but I speedily
found I was mistaken. The snails took, and the
"highest quality" of the city of Lyons came flocking to
the Rue St. Dominique to pay four shillings for a dish
of snails. Would they have patronised the place at
thirty sous? I am inclined to doubt it.

I can recommend the following way of preparing a
savoury dish of tripe: Chop an ounce of parsley and
of tarragon, half an ounce of savory and lemon thyme
mixed, two ounces of mushrooms, a tablespoonful of
capers, and two anchovies boned. Put them in a stew-
pan with half a pint of French vinegar, a pint and a
half of water, half an ounce of salt; add a dozen white
peppercorns, twelve cloves, a few blades of mace, a nutmeg grated, the peel of a lemon grated, the juice of the
lemon, two spoonfuls of ketchup, and two glasses of
white wine. Set the pan over a slow fire, and let the
contents simmer about an hour. Meanwhile prepare

your tripe. This you get ready dressed, and with the coarser part of the fat removed by the tripe seller. Put two pounds of it ten minutes in boiling water. Cut it into neat small pieces, and fry them a light yellow in six ounces of boiling butter. Set them aside in a dish. Fry in the same butter four ounces of onions cut in thin slices. Add the tripe, onions and butter to the stew in the pan, and let it boil another quarter of an hour. This recipe is based in a measure upon a way of preparing tripe which they have in Normandy. *Tripe à la mode de Caen,* they call it.

I once upon a time prepared a dish of tripe after this fashion for some of my most intimate friends—the late T. W. Robertson among them. It was before the days of "Society." The delicate dish took amazingly, and I was asked for my recipe. I gave it. James Lowe, Halliday, and John Brough wrote it down *séance tenante.* Robertson seemed plunged in a brown study. "What is the matter with you, Robertson? What are you thinking of?" I cried. "Thinking of?" he replied, slowly and ponderously. "Why, I am thinking I would as lief forswear tripe altogether as to incur the expense and trouble to make it palatable." I was taken down considerably—particularly when I saw Andrew Halliday tear up *his* copy of the recipe. "The bearing of this lies in the application of it," says the great Mariner Busby.

Another dear friend of mine, who, also, has long since joined the majority, was very fond of my tripe *à la mode de Caen.* He had the germ of consumption in him, and was advised by the late Dr. Ramadge to visit the South of France. He went to Cannes, and took up his quarters there at a swell hotel. Mindful of my great dish, he innocently ordered tripe for dinner, pleasantly remarking that, as he was now at the fountain head of the article, he expected to have it first-rate. He told me, after his return to London, that to say the proprietor of the place was fiercely indignant would be to put it in a very mild way. The idea of ordering tripe at a Cannes *hôtel de premier rang!* it was an insult. My poor friend was deterred from asking the man what made him so angry.

I have ventured to mention among comestibles the ESCARGOT, or large gray shell snail, which is generally classed with lizards and snakes and other foods that are held to be of a somewhat disgusting nature. There is a strong prejudice in England against snails, no matter *how* cooked and prepared. Yet the snail was at one time held in great estimation as a light and most easily digested food for the sick, especially the consumptive. Even in my own time I have seen it ordered and eaten in England in a vinous stew—chablis or hock—with Iceland moss and laver, grated nutmeg and lemon juice. The snails are prepared by throwing them into boiling salt water, letting them boil an hour, then drawing them from their shells with a fork, stripping off the black membrane, &c., and strewing a handful of salt over them to detach the slime, washing them four or five times in warm water, squeezing the water out, boiling them soft in good broth, then chopping them fine, and mixing the minced mass ultimately with the laver and moss.

I have eaten snails in several forms, and I can truthfully affirm that they are by no means bad eating in form of soup, or salad, or served in their shells with stuffing. The only valid drawback, in fact, that I can see to their use for food is that they do not contain much nutriment. I am sadly afraid, however, that I shall bring not a few anathemas on my devoted head by boldly daring to give a few snail recipes here. " Strike! but hear! " exclaimed Themistocles to the irate Spartan—" Scold! but try! " cry I to the impatient reader.

For SNAIL SOUP prepare your snails as above. Boil fifty washed and squeezed out snails soft in good broth, take them out and chop two-thirds very fine, stew them a little in butter, add as much of the broth as may be required for the soup, season with a few blades of mace, let it boil up repeatedly, and stir in a few yolks of egg. Pour the soup over some rounds of toast and the remaining third part of the snails.

To make a SNAIL SALAD, slice your snails, properly prepared and boiled, lengthways, and mix them with the quantity needed of salt, ground pepper, finely chopped shalots, chervil and tarragon, and two parts of fine salad oil to one part of French vinegar.

STUFFED SNAILS served in their shells are done as follows:—Prepare your snails as before, and wash and dry the shells thoroughly. Chop four anchovies, washed and boned, with half an ounce of parsley, add a little mace and white pepper. Add a large tablespoonful of grated bread, a teaspoonful of flour and two ounces and a half of butter, and mix thoroughly, with kneading. Put into each shell a small portion of this stuffing, then a snail, and finally some more stuffing. Arrange the shells in a saucepan side by side, with the opening turned upwards, pour a large ladleful of broth over them, boil a quarter of an hour, and serve in form of a pyramid, with four hard boiled eggs cut in four at the base, sprinkled over with salt and pepper.

The third and last of these exceptional viands—the FROG—I approach more diffidently even than the snail. I know not how to account for it, but frogs have more than once in my life been the cause of serious trouble to me.

Many years ago, when I was living at Dijon, I was peregrinating one day about Fontaine. I came to a pond where several men and boys were engaged in

taking frogs. As a rule they dashed the poor animals
on a stone, then cut off or tore out the hind legs.
There were two or three young villains there who
evidently thought it too much trouble to kill the frogs,
but contented themselves with pulling away the legs
and throwing the wretched frogs back into the pond
alive. I could not stand this horrible cruelty. As my
remonstrances were of no avail, I boxed the ears of
one of the young scamps. Immediately the whole
band set upon me, and I had to fight hard for it. Had
it not been for the accidental appearance on the scene
of a *garde champêtre,* these wretches might have
murdered me, but the instant they caught sight of
authority in a cocked hat and with a sabre, they caved
in, and tried to run for it. It was no go, however, the
garde champêtre knew them, and they had to appear
at Fontaine next morning, where they owed their escape
from punishment for *voies de fait* on the public road
only to my intercession.

In 1875 I was in Strasburg. I went to the Ostrich
Hotel and Restaurant, intent upon baked frog legs.
Seeing a young woman of rather tallish and thinnish
appearance standing near the *comptoir,* I thought she
belonged to the place, and innocently asked her,
"Fräulein, haben Sie Froschschenkel?"—"Miss, have
you frog legs?" Now the young woman was simply
a visitor to the place, and she mistook my inquiry for

a slighting reflection upon her understandings. No
explanation, no apology would avail me. The young
termagant fell upon me with her tongue, and tried her
very worst to be at me with her nails in my face. Her
mother came up to the aid of her insulted child, and
threatened to shake the life out of mé. At last they
actually brought me before the *Juge de Paix*, a dull
German, who could not see the alleged insult, and fined
the prosecutrix five francs for bringing me there upon
a trumpery charge.

After this reminiscential digression, I crave permission to give two recipes, the one how to bake the hind
legs of the frog, the other how to make tasty ragout of
them.

Put the hind legs in a suitable vessel with a mixture
in equal parts—according to requirement—of water
and French vinegar, to which add a handful of salt.
Whip the legs about with a broom, to thoroughly cleanse
them, and wash them in several waters. Melt one to
two ounces of butter in a saucepan, and lay in the frog
legs, a few shalots in thin slices, and a little salt, put
on the lid tight and stew over a slow fire until nearly
done. Then dredge a little flour over the stew, add a
pint—more or less, according to requirement—of strong
broth, a lemon sliced, with the peel and the pips removed,
a few blades of nutmeg, a tablespoonful of ketchup and
one of Worcester sauce, and keep the stew simmering

until the legs are quite done and tender. Whip the sauce up with the yolks of one or two raw eggs, and serve hot. I am told that the edible frog is now occasionally imported from France alive. The easiest and least painful way to kill a frog is to give it a hard blow on the head with a heavy hammer.

To BAKE frog legs, clean and wash them as directed, sprinkle salt over them, and let them stand a quarter of an hour; then wash them in cold water, dry them in a clean cloth, dip them in butter seasoned with grated nutmeg, roll them in pounded biscuit (which, of course, must not be sweet), and bake them yellow—about a quarter of an hour—in hot melted butter.

PART V.

VEGETABLES

FRESH VEGETABLES are an indispensable adjunct to a wholesome table. Deprivation of them for any notable length of time is incompatible with the preservation of health. The most distressing and fatal disease that afflicts sailors on long sea voyages—the scurvy—is caused chiefly, if not entirely, by the prolonged absence of fresh vegetables from their diet. The addition of a pound of potatoes to their daily food acts as the most effectual preventive of that dread malady.

It has often been observed that no country produces better esculent vegetables than England, because in no other land are vegetables so carefully cultivated; and it must, in common fairness, be admitted that the observation holds good within by no means narrow limits. However, there is a rider to the general statement, to wit, that the superiority of our vegetables is not permitted to pass the threshold of our kitchen doors, and that in the crude state in which we somehow seem to persist in placing them on our tables they cannot possibly be expected to properly fulfil their intended functions, but that they are rather much more likely to cause indigestion and even confirmed dyspepsia. On the continent they steer clear of this inconvenience by simply looking upon vegetables as separate and distinct foods, not mere adjuncts to meat, and making them accordingly into palatable independent dishes. They use butter on the continent, or lard, dripping, goose fat, duck fat, suet, rendered with milk, and mutton fat (from young animals only), also melted with milk, for the preparation of palatable vegetable dishes. These fats must be absolutely free from all albumenoid or other admixture. They should be kept in stone jars, tied over with perforated paper, in a cool and airy place. If the least taint is observed in a fat, it should at once be re-melted.

Fresh vegetables, especially of the cabbage tribe, should be put at once into fast boiling water, in small successive portions, to prevent stopping of the boiling. Salt should be added only towards the end of the cooking, as its earlier application would simply tend to harden the vegetables. They should also be boiled in open pans, to prevent the return of the parts driven off by the heat. Boiling water should always be kept at hand, to re-fill in case of need.

POTATOES also, whether new or old, should be put at once in fast boiling water, and salt should be added only about five minutes before the end of the process. The Chinese, who certainly are very good cooks as a rule, do their potatoes in boiling water.

I always boil my potatoes *open*. I do not wish to speak *ex cathedrâ*, but I must say I find them most palatable done that way. I object altogether to steaming potatoes. This vegetable contains a peculiar substance of nauseous taste, which is driven off by the heat in the process of cooking. Now, in steaming potatoes, not alone does the condensed steam run back into the saucepan underneath, imparting an unpleasant flavour to any other vegetable being boiled in it, but it passes also through the potatoes again, impairing their flavour. For this reason, M. TEGETMEIER contends that potatoes intended for an Irish stew or for soup should be boiled by themselves first, and the water thrown away.

M. TEGETMEIER also says potatoes should be cooked with their skins on, except when baked under meat; for if peeled before boiling there is great waste as well as considerable loss of time. Unpeeled potatoes can also be cooked to a much higher degree of perfection than the pared tubers. I most fully concur with him in both views.

If you think you *must* peel your potatoes, peel them only just when you want to put them into the boiling water. To keep the peeled potato soaking in cold water for an indefinite time is apt to lead to the extraction of an undue proportion of the fecula and the salts.

In boiling potatoes, peeled and unpeeled, you should always take care to have your tubers as nearly as practicable of the same size. Do not throw them in all at once, but lay the largest at the bottom, the smallest at the top, and put them in gradually to give the water time to keep on boiling with the least possible interruption. Never boil your potatoes before you want them. "From the fire to the table" should be your motto. Never cover them over when they are done. The same rule applies to all fresh vegetables.

No time can be specified for boiling vegetables tender. The time depends upon the kind, nature, and age of the vegetable. In dry seasons more time is required than in wet seasons.

New potatoes will take fifteen to twenty minutes to boil tender. When they get older more time is required. It is said that potatoes in April require fully three quarters of an hour to one hour even, to be properly done. I have always found thirty to forty minutes sufficient, even in May. Never try your potatoes with the fork long before they can possibly be done. It is apt to spoil them, causing them to break and crumble.

Never send broken potatoes to the table, but use

them for stews and soups, or mash them with milk and lard or butter, or, best of all, pork dripping, working through the mash in the saucepan a shalot or two, and some parsley, both finely chopped, and seasoning with salt and pepper, according to requirement. Set the saucepan over a clear fire or on the gas stove, and keep stirring until the mash is thoroughly mixed and heated through. I may remark here that one of the most frequent causes of broken potatoes is the repeated prodding with a fork to try whether they are done. If you put your potatoes in boiling water and keep them properly boiling for the time personal experience will soon teach you to fix, a single try will suffice. Potatoes properly boiled, and just ready for the table at the proper time, are sure to be done in every way, colour included, to a high point of perfection.

The seeds of leguminous plants—more particularly those that come under our more immediate consideration here—peas, lentils, and beans, to wit, rank with the highest albumenoid foods, and ought certainly to command a wider sphere of consumption than is allotted to them in England, where their use in the dried state has for the last forty years or so shewn an increasing tendency to decrease, more especially that of the dried pea, which requires long soaking to soften the skin for its ultimate indispensable rejection. The skin of the haricot bean is more easily detached. The lentil is very rarely seen in this country—mostly in foreign provision stores and dining rooms, or in powder, as "Revalenta," for the use of invalids, strangely enough, who must often find it difficult to digest it. The lentil is rather a nice tasted seed, though the flavour is by no means universally liked. Esau sold his birthright to his crafty brother for a mess of lentils. He must have been literally starving at the time, otherwise it is difficult to account for such a very extraordinary bargain.

Haricot beans are eaten in the pod in the mature state. Boiled and tossed in a pan with butter or lard and a sprinkle of salt they are excellent eating. The pods of the haricot and scarlet runner are cut into thin slices and boiled, with a little salt added three or four minutes before they are taken off the fire. They are accounted a delicate dish, by no means difficult to digest.

Green beans should always be *most carefully* stringed. Where the strings are not properly removed, the dish is spoiled.

Sweet peas should never be bought ready shelled, unless the purchaser has good reason to believe that it is not likely a mixture of new and old, fresh and stale, will be palmed upon him. It is wise also to buy such peas only as have been brought to market in wicker baskets, through which the air has free circulation. Peas imported in close sacks are ever apt to get heated and to ferment, which, of course, renders their use for food unwholesome.

When green peas are going out of season, they lose the agreeable sweetness of the earlier supplies. This may be restored, to some extent at least, by adding a lump of sugar to the water in which they are to be boiled.

Green peas are done and eaten to perfection only when fresh gathered—from cutting to cooking, from the garden to the kitchen. At least they should be sold and bought fresh in the market on the morning of their arrival from the country. Every housekeeper should make it a point to deal only with traders of good repute, whose fair fame is a guarantee for their fair dealing.

The pea played an important part in the Franco-German War of 1870—71.

That the purveying and victualling department must always claim a paramount share of attention and care on the part of the leaders of an army in the field is a self-evident preposition. At the outbreak of that war, GRÜNBERG, a culinary artist of Berlin, devised a savory and nutritious preserve for the German army in the field—the pea sausage, consisting, as compounded by him, of pea meal, best beef suet, bacon (two parts of lean to one of fat), onions, salt, and spices, fitted into paper cases specially prepared for the purpose, in which the sausage will keep unaltered for years in any place After the war a private German soldier sang the praises of this most valuable comestible in a special line, proclaiming the special share of the pea sausage in the great success. The Prussian Government made the fortunate inventor a present of £10,000, and had a manufactory of the article built at Berlin at the cost of the State. Towards the close of the war some 150,000 pounds of pea sausage were daily produced at this establishment, 2,400 males and females being employed in the production of this large supply.

All green vegetables should be cooked in soft water Addition of a small lump of soda will preserve the fresh green colour. Always boil your fresh vegetables uncovered, and do not get them done before they are required, as exposure to the air tends to impair their flavour. The advice to have your vegetables always only just done when they are required on the table may seem useless reiteration; but it is of the highest importance and cannot be too strongly insisted upon.

Vegetables preserved in tins, &c., will do when the fresh articles are out of season, or beyond reach of slender purses. It should be borne in mind, however, that it is unreasonable to expect to find perfect substitutes in them. Preserved vegetables are not fresh vegetables. This may look a trivial remark to make, but it is most true. I will admit, however, that I have

occasionally tasted tinned French beans and green peas
that came within measurable distance of the fresh
plants. I have tried a large variety of asparagus in
tins and glasses, but I have found most of them lamentably wanting. I must make an exception, however,
in favour of the so-called Oyster Bay asparagus, imported from America, which I have found very good,
and certainly worth the money, 1s. 4d. I think, for
sixty to seventy stalks. A dram of salt, two tablespoonfuls of vinegar, three of oil, and a dash of Worcester,
make an excellent sauce for asparagus, no matter whether
fresh or preserved. The same sauce will do for artichokes.
Although containing from above eighty to ninety per
cent. of water, all the plants of the cabbage tribe are excellent food, the solid part consisting chiefly of albumenoid
substances. As the plants of the cabbage tribe contain
no fatty matter they should be eaten, preferentially,
with fat bacon, &c., after the French fashion.

ONIONS and SHALOTS are always better for being
shredded or chopped fine, even where intended for
frying or for flavouring stews, soups, &c. Still more so
where they are to be eaten uncooked, as in salads, &c.,
as they are by no means easily digested in that state,
and comminution acts as a most powerful aid to digestion. Garlic I number among the condiments.

TOMATOS are used chiefly in the form of a very pleasing subacid sauce. My way of preparing this is simply

as follows:—Pour boiling water over the tomatos, and peel the skin off—shred the tomatos pretty fine—I do not remove the kernels or pips, as I do not find them to interfere injuriously with the quality and taste of the sauce—boil them in good stock or broth mixed with a teaspoonful of Liebig's extract. Blend a teaspoonful of flour with part of the broth, add the juice of half a lemon and a tablespoonful of Worcester sauce, and stir the paste in the boiling sauce. Season with salt, and dilute to the proper consistency with the stock or broth at hand.

The English recipe directs the removal of the kernels or pips.

The German recipe tells you to dry your tomatos, cut them in pieces, boil them rapidly in water, then in a little broth, pass them through a tamis; melt a couple of ounces of butter, and blend a teaspoonful or so of flour in it over a brisk fire to a fine yellow tint. Put the tomatos in, and boil with broth until perfectly done. Season with a little grated nutmeg.

SOURCROUT is by many, even in England, considered an excellent dish. It should be made of summer cabbage. Winter cabbage sourcrout is always apt to be toughish. There are three places in Germany that share among them the reputation of making and exporting the best sourcrout—Lauenburg, to wit, Magdeburg, and Strasburg. The crout made in Magdeburg, with Borsdorf pippins, is held to be the best. Sourcrout may

M

be readily procured in London, as all German provision
dealers import it.   Put a pound or two of the article in
a suitable stone jar, with slices of fat bacon at the
bottom and in alternate layers.   Place the jar in a
moderately hot oven, and let it stew from five to six
hours.   Serve with Frankfurt sausages, or boiled ham
or pork, or corned beef.

In Germany they stew sourcrout occasionally with a
mixture in equal parts of butter, lard, and beef suet;
also, for the sake of economy, with lard and rape seed
oil mixed.   I must say I admire neither way, though I, of
course, would prefer the former, if driven to adopt either.

A dear friend of mine, a gentleman of the Hebrew
persuasion, most liberal minded, is very fond of Frankfurt sausages and sourcrout.   He maintains that the
sausages are made of beef.   You may also line the
jar (bottom and sides) with rashers of fat bacon.   Put
in half a pound of sourcrout, then a sausage, then a
quarter pound of sourcrout, another sausage, and so on
to the top, and let it stew gently till done.   To do
Frankfurt sausages by themselves to perfection, heat
water in a saucepan to fast boiling; then put in your
sausages, and let them boil eight minutes.   Serve with
the sourcrout, or with horseradish sauce, or with
mashed potatoes.

Of CUCUMBERS I shall have occasion to speak in the
chapter specially devoted to salads.

A succulent dish may be made of vegetable marrow, stuffed with meat, as follows. Cut a large marrow lengthways in two, hollow the halves out, and fill in pork and veal, and one or two shalots, finely chopped, with a seasoning of sweet herbs, grated lemon peel, pepper, salt, grated nutmeg, and a little lemon juice. Tie the two halves together, and stew over a slow fire, or on the hot plate.

I would, indeed, have liked to say something here on the important branches of SOUPS and SAUCES, OMELETTES, PANCAKES, and other EGG and MILK and CREAM preparations; PIES, PUDDINGS, PASTRY, CAKES, JELLIES, FRUITS, &c., but that I feel it would be travelling beyond the scope and purpose of this little book, as explained in the introductory part. Besides, these branches are treated more or less exhaustively in all good cookery books, to which the reader may, therefore, safely be referred.

I have, however, a few general remarks to append on CONDIMENTS, SALADS, UNFERMENTED BEVERAGES, and FERMENTED DRINKS, which I proceed to do in a

SPECIAL APPENDIX.

I.

CONDIMENTS.

THE most important condiments are salt, vinegar, pepper and spices, and seasoning herbs, &c. Properly speaking, they are rather adjuncts to food than aliments in themselves ; many of them may be looked upon also as medicinal agents. Their principal function, however, is to render food more palatable, stimulate a jaded appetite, promote digestion, and assist materially in the preservation of food.

The chief condiment of all has been through all ages SALT, which truly is not simply an adjunct to food, or a mere useful stimulant, but a necessary of life, each person requiring a quarter to half an ounce daily for the preservation of health, and even of life. Of this quantity part only is contained in our food and drink, the balance wanted having to be supplied from other

direct sources out of nature's immense store-house. In
the course of a long life and most varied experience, I
have only met one man who found the salt contained in
his food and drink sufficient to keep him in health, and
who never took a grain of salt with his food. This was
my dear friend Watkins, late of Falcon Square, the
famous healer of gout and rheumatism, and a host of
kindred ailments, now long since gone to the place
where he must have found his " occupation gone " too
He was an excellent physician and a sound thinker in
the main, albeit somewhat eccentric. It was his special
craze to look upon the use of salt as the great mistake
of the human race, the *fons et origo malorum!* He
seemed somehow to have a notion that the patriarchs
owed their astonishing longevity simply to the fact that
salt had not yet been discovered in their time. However, he was in this respect a most exceptional exception
indeed.

SALT, or CHLORIDE OF SODIUM, taken in food supplies
the material of two of the most powerful agents in the
processes of digestion and nutrition—the gastric juice,
to wit, and the bile.

There is implanted in man and the animals alike an
instinctive craving for salt. Astute governments have
often taken advantage of the indispensability of salt to
extort literally a life tax from the very poorest, who
would, it was shrewdly held, make almost any sacrifice

to obtain this precious matter so necessary to health and life.*

At this present time every one, at least in the British Isles, may command an almost unlimited supply of salt, which also has its drawback. We are apt to use this great blessing in excess. It may be laid down as a safe rule for the kitchen and table that undersalting is less inconvenient, and less likely to be hurtful, than oversalting. You can always add to a deficient quantity of salt, whilst you cannot take the excess away. Of course I am perfectly aware that there are many ways and methods and processes recommended by the ingenious to effect this desirable end, and there may certainly be some of these more or less effectual ; only, I am sorry to say, my personal experience in this matter makes me slightly doubtful of this.

In cookery instructions no general quantitative rules can well be laid down for the use of salt. Experience

---

* Our actual "taxers" would seem to act upon a similar notion with regard to beer and spirits, in attempting to raise still higher an already exorbitant tax. They may chance to find their notion a very serious mistake and blunder. It would be better for the revenue and for the cause of temperance to lower the duty and to put down by the strong hand of the *criminal* law the infamous adulteration of wine, beer, and spirits, which forms one of the blackest plague spots of our time. Were our fermented liquors but pure there would not be half, nay, not a fourth, the intemperance which we have to deplore at present.

is the best guide in this, as in many other questions of proper proportions.

Its affinity for water makes salt a great preserving agent for meat and other substances; putrefaction requiring the presence of moisture, which salt absorbs. The use of salt in the preservation of meat has been spoken of already, and commented upon in the proper place. In some countries, as in France and Germany, for instance, salt is largely employed for the preservation of green vegetables for use in winter.

VINEGAR also is a favourite condiment, and a powerful agent of preservation. It has the faculty of softening the fibres of meat, and making them tender. It may be derived from a variety of sources, as all saccharine matters are capable of acetous fermentation ; and in former times, when it was by no means easy to get good vinegar everywhere at a moderate price, it was often made at home from weak solutions of sugar, with or without the aid of the so-called vinegar plant. Now-a-days, this is no longer necessary, or even profitable, as good grape vinegar—the best of the class—can be procured at the moderate price of eight to ten pence per bottle. Malt vinegar may also be got at a similar price, but it is an inferior article to grape vinegar. The true vinegar acid is acetic acid ; but, unhappily, hydro-chloric and sulphuric acids are often used to "fortify" the pure article. Adulteration with the former may be detected by addition of nitrate of silver, with the latter by adding chloride of barium. A white deposit is proof positive of the presence of the one or the other of these acids.

Vinegar forms the foundation of many sauces and a variety of pickles. It is often used flavoured with garlic, tarragon, mint, and other herbs, &c.

To make GARLIC VINEGAR, pull your garlic any time between June and September—August answers best. Chop two or three ounces very fine, and tie them in a small muslin bag. Suspend this in a well stoppered quart jar, and fill up with best French vinegar, with two ounces of salt dissolved in it. Put the stopper in tight, and let the jar stand a full fortnight to three weeks, shaking it well every day except the last two days, to allow any floating impurities to subside. Then decant the clear liquid and strain or filter into small bottles. Cork the bottles well. This acetic essence of garlic is very powerful, and should be used most sparingly and with proper judgment. So subtle and penetrating is the flavour that a few drops of the essence will be found amply sufficient to impart to broth, gravies, soups, ragouts, and salads, that delicate suspicion of the presence of garlic which the French call *soupçon d'ail;* whilst the least excess in its use may spoil the finest and most tasty dish.

SHALOT VINEGAR may be prepared in the same way.

TARRAGON, the same as other HERBAL VINEGARS, can only be made with fresh leaves, June and August being the two best months for tarragon. Gather your leaves fresh and green on a dry day, just before the herb flowers. Pick them off the stalks, and put them at once *unwashed* into a wide-mouthed well-stoppered bottle—four to six ounces will do. Fill the bottle with the best French vinegar, and put the stopper in tight. Prepare in this way as many bottles as you think you may require, and place them a fortnight in the sun. Decant and strain or filter into small bottles, which cork well and keep in a dry place.

MINT, BASIL, and other HERBAL VINEGARS may be made pretty much in the same way. The middle of August is the best time for making basil vinegar. Never use dried leaves for herbal vinegars.

LEMONS may be classed with CONDIMENTS. They play an important part in cookery. The juice is not unfrequently used as a refined substitute for vinegar, as in the preparation of delicate mint sauce, for instance; occasionally also as an agreeable and improving adjunct to vinegar. The use of the rind or peel, grated or chopped, also pervades, more or less, almost all the more delicate culinary processes. Grating the rind is not a good or profitable way to get the largest practically obtainable amount of the essence from the lemon. To succeed in this, pare your lemon with a sharp small

knife, taking care to cut right through the many cells
containing the essence, without encroaching on the
white part of the rind. The essence remaining in the
latter may be got away readily by rubbing with a lump
of sugar. The outer yellow shaving ought to be chopped
fine. If you have to cut the lemon in slices or disks,
always take care to strip off the pulpy white part, and
to remove the pips, as both are disagreeably bitter.

Essence or oil of lemon will be found a most practical
and advantageous substitute for fresh lemon peel, which
is by no means an article to be relied upon for a uniform
quantity of oil, as some lemons are abundantly supplied
with it, whilst others are dry rinded, and contain hardly
any essence.

One part of best essential oil of lemon is dissolved in
sixteen parts of pure alcohol, the latter being added
gradually to the former until complete solution is
effected.

GARLIC is a most excellent condiment. Only, as has
been said already in the paragraph on garlic vinegar,
it must be used judiciously and sparingly. There are
many people who really like the flavour of that bulb,
yet abstain from it simply because they are afraid it
may inconveniently affect them—and many plans have
been devised to take away what may be called the
objectionable properties of this condiment. I remember—I think it must be more than forty years ago

now—that a high gastronomic authority in those days, the Editor of the *Magazine of Domestic Economy,* sagely advised the readers of that wondrous repository of culinary lore to boil their garlic five minutes in water, and to repeat the same operation *six* times in different waters; when they would find that it had entirely lost its objectionable properties. So it will, of course, as any of my readers may try, only the bulb treated in this fashion will be found to have absolutely ceased to be garlic. Horseradish, another condiment, has the objectionable knack to affect the mucous membrane of the nose, and to draw scalding tears from the eyes. Boil a stick of horseradish in six different waters, and dry it in a hot oven, and I am quite sure you may scrape it afterwards without inconvenience to your nostrils and eyes.

The largest and most important class of condiments, however, is formed by peppers and spices—black pepper, to wit, and Jamaica pepper, or Pimento; nutmeg and mace; coriander, cumin, cardamom, and mustard seeds; cayenne and chillies; cloves and cinnamon; bay and laurel leaves; tarragon, spearmint, peppermint, sage, marjoram, thyme, and other garden herbs; ginger, &c., &c.

PEPPER is the seed or berry of the black pepper shrub—*Piper nigrum.* Many people will insist upon the existence of two distinct shrubs—the black and the

white, and hold the latter vastly superior to the former.
This is a popular error, which it is sometimes found
difficult to combat successfully. The berry of the
pepper shrub has a dark brown or black cuticle, and it
is the removal or non-removal of this skin which makes
the sole difference between black pepper and white
pepper, and connoisseurs look upon the black as the
superior article of the two.

Many long years ago, when I was at Lyons, I was
intimately acquainted with M. de S., a wealthy silk
manufacturer. I had occasion, at the time, to recommend to Madame S. for cook an exceptionally well-
educated young Alsatian. The girl was engaged, and
everything went well for some months, when I was
unexpectedly informed by Madame that she was
compelled to part with her cook, as she seemed
inclined to *cheek* her. "Sir," the lady said, with considerable irritation, "she had the impertinence to tell
me that black pepper was the same as white pepper,
and she persists in that absurd assertion, though M. de
S. has seriously remonstrated with her." Well—well,
I made the poor girl apologise for her presumption and
ignorance, and she kept her place. Never presume to
know better than your "betters" is a sound old
maxim.

There is another of the condimentary seeds which
presents two varieties, a black or brown and a white—

MUSTARD to wit. But in this case the distinction is with a difference, the black or brown seeds containing a volatile pungent, the white a fixed acrid principle.

MUSTARD is one of the oldest condiments known. The Romans—who got it originally from Egypt, where it had been in common use from the most remote times —prepared it for the table with the unfermented juice of the grape—the must. Hence it was called by them *mustum ardens* (hot must), from which term the French word "*moutarde*" and the English "*mustard*" are derived.

Many years ago, when temporarily engaged in making table mustard at Dijon, I made experiments with must, with results not wholly unsatisfactory, as I have reason to believe that some, at least, of the *moutarde de Dijon*, exported at the time from the capital of Burgundy, was made in the Roman fashion. This *mustum ardens* was brought to England by the Roman invaders, and taken kindly to by the natives, it would appear, and by the several nations that landed subsequently on our shores on the same invasive errand. We have it on record that in the fourteenth century it was used in England as a favourite condiment, mixed with honey, vinegar, and wine. It is largely grown in England, the black variety—*sinapis nigra*—principally in the vicinity of Wisbeach; the white variety—*sinapis alba*—chiefly in Essex and Cambridge. There are extensive manufactories of table mustard, where the seeds are crushed to press out the fixed oil, then ground to an impalpable powder. The flour of the black seed is far more pungent, of course, than that of the white seed, as it contains the volatile principle. It is even held necessary to mix the two seeds together in certain proportions, that the excessive pungency of the black may be mitigated by the admixture of the white. Even this is considered insufficient for the purpose, and flour is generally also added to prepare table mustard for the market, which sometimes, unhappily, leads to an excessive weakening of the condiment, and to the addition of capsicum to make up for the deficiency; but capsicum cannot replace the volatile principle of the black seed.

The article thus adulterated is no longer mustard in the proper sense of the term. There are, however, fortunately, large manufactories of table mustard in England where the article is prepared in a state of absolute purity, or, to suit the taste of consumers, with a certain admixture of the finest wheaten flour, and perhaps, a very minute proportion of turmeric. The price of the black seed rules generally some twenty per cent. or so higher than that of the white seed.

Mustard for the table is made in England, as a general rule, in a very simple way. A quarter of a pound of mustard is mixed with one ounce of salt, and the mixture stirred and blended with five tablespoonfuls of water. When the paste is perfectly smooth, another tablespoonful of water is added, and the mixture again well blended. If the first material is pure, this mustard is most pungent. I think it is the preparation dispensed generally in ham and beef shops. The taste is a little crude perhaps, and acrid, as it is mostly made of a mixture of equal parts of the two seeds, and contains no flavouring, except the salt added. Still, where there is a brisk demand for it this way of its preparation for the table is by no means bad or extravagant. But it will not keep long, the pungency soon going off, so that, as will often happen in small families, a more or less notable portion may have to be thrown away. Some use boiling water, which will bring out the pungency faster, but with this drawback that it also goes off much sooner. Taking this into due account, the article made simply with salt and water may cost dearer in the end than the more agreeably flavoured table mustards imported from France and Germany, which on their part, however, labour under the notable disadvantage of lack of pungency, owing to the mode of their manufacture.

England imports ready made mustard largely from France and Germany, in jars and glasses—chiefly from Bordeaux, Dijon, and Düsseldorf.

In private families in Germany, table mustard is

prepared in various ways. Some mix, say half a pound of mustard flour, as supplied by the makers, with one ounce of pounded sugar, and work and blend this with cold water to a stiff, smooth paste, which is then diluted to the desired consistency required by adding vinegar, flavoured generally with garlic or anchovy, or some aromatic herb, &c. Others use boiling water instead of cold, which in my opinion is certainly not the most economical way.

I have dabbled in mustard making for half a century, and many are the large jars, and many, many more still the small jars I have in that time prepared for my friends and my own use.

When I have all appliances required at hand, I proceed in an apparently somewhat complicated way, which I will here briefly describe in form of a recipe:—Take six ounces of black mustard seed—*Sinapis nigra*—three ounces of the white—*Sinapis alba*—place them separately on a couple of sheets of paper, and let them dry in a moderately heated oven. When quite dry grind them separately in a sharp set seed mill, or pound them (separately) in a mortar. Add to the black seed powder one ounce of salt and one of pounded sugar, with two teaspoonfuls of Harvey, Worcester, or some other sauce of the kind, and work and blend the mixture to a stiff smooth paste with the requisite quantity of water—say six tablespoonfuls, more or less

as you may find needful. Mix the white seed powder
with about four tablespoonfuls, more or less according
to requirement, of viuegar flavoured with garlic, or
tarragon, anchovy, basil, mint, &c., as stated in the
paragraph on vinegar, and blend the mass to a smooth
paste. Then mix the two pastes together, and transfer
the whole to a well stoppered glass or stone jar—or
better still, to a French plum jar with over-lapping
screw cover—and keep in a cool place. The mustard
is ready for the table in a few days, and will keep for
months with a little care to have the jar always well
closed. It is most pungent, and a small portion of it
will go a long way; although the fixed oil being left in
it tends to mellow its sharpness.

When I was in Paris in 1864, I made a jar of it for
the proprietor of the *Café de la Tour St. Jacques.*
Among the habitués of the place was a Breton gentleman, who was passionately addicted to eating mustard
on bread and butter, and who would occasionally take
a teaspoonful of *Moutarde de Maille* neat by way of
an appetizer. He wished to try my production. I duly
cautioned him; I entreated him to make an essay with a
very little on the top of his finger. He scorned the
notion, and with the obstinacy of a Breton, he *would*
have his way. Well, he *had* his way—and he jumped
about like one possessed, shouting and swearing at me,
calling me an assassin, and threatening to have my life.

N

We succeeded at last in appeasing his wrath, and after all he took kindly to my mustard, and wheedled the receipt out of me.

The reason for the separate treatment of the two seeds—the one with water, the other with vinegar—instead of mixing the two at once, and treating the mixture with vinegar and water, is simply that water is a more efficacious agent for the rapid evolution of the volatile principle of the black seed than a mixture of vinegar and water, whilst the unwatered vinegar seems to me better suited to act upon the fixed acrid principle of the white seed. I frankly admit, however, that there may be some fancy in this notion, at least, I know that very good table mustard may be made without strictly adhering to the above prescription anent the separate treatment of the two seeds. In fact, I can only rarely command all the appliances required, more especially a good seed mill, and I am thus often compelled to have recourse to a modification of the process, in which I deal with the manufactured mustard powder direct. I have now for some forty-five years used Keen's mustard in this modified process, and I must say I have invariably found this preparation most fully up to the mark, and perfectly pure in every way. To prepare it for the table, take, say eight ounces of it, add one ounce of salt, and one of pounded sugar, with two teaspoonfuls of sauce (Harvey, Worcester, &c.), and mix with the requisite quantity of water to a stiff, smooth paste. Give a little time, say a quarter of an hour, to set the evolution of the volatile principle going, then stir in the quantity of vinegar (Tarragon, &c.) required to bring the mass to the proper consistency, which must never be less than will let the mixing spatula stand upright in it. Bear in mind that wood is the safest material for the mustard spatula and spoon. Metals should be carefully avoided, and horn is destructively affected by acids. Transfer the made mustard to a glass jar with tight stopper, or to a French plum jar with over-lapping screw cover. I generally put on the mustard in the jar a paper disk of exactly corresponding size, brushed over with a little sweet oil, and dipped subsequently into boiling syrup, which serves to shield the contents of the jar from contact with the air. I may say here, *en passant*, that these disks will answer equally well for preserves, &c. Set the jar in a cool place; the mustard will keep for months. Whenever you take out a portion for use, smooth the surface of what is left in the jar, and replace or renew the protecting disk. Freshen the part taken out for use with a little water, which will serve to bring out the pungency.

TURMERIC is the dried tuber of *Curcuma longa*, which is extensively grown in the East Indies, where it is largely used as a condiment, more especially in the preparation of CURRIE POWDER, into the composition of which it enters to the extent of one clear half to three-fifths. It is ground to a fine powder before use. I have now lying before me an East Indian recipe, which fixes the proportion of turmeric at thirteeen ounces in twenty-four, the other ingredients being cumin and coriander two ounces and a half each, cardamon and caraway seeds one ounce each, half an ounce of fenugreek, one ounce and a quarter of cayenne, three quarters of an ounce each of black pepper, pimento and cloves. Other recipes counsel the addition of green ginger, cinnamon, mace, and rasped cocoanut pulp. Excellent currie powder is to be had in England of most grocers. However, for the benefit of those inclined to have something special of their own make, I subjoin a recipe, the essential and distinguishing feature of which I gratefully acknowledge to owe to the same friend to whom I am indebted for the capital hint about the flour in pancakes (see page 86), Mr. Linford, of Hull.

Take three-quarter of an ounce each of ground black pepper, pimento and cloves, and grated nutmeg, half an ounce of cayenne—which is amply sufficient—and twelve ounces of turmeric, and mix these ingredients well together. Now for the essential feature of the process, which consists in this:—Instead of using the ordinary mill ground powders of the seeds of cumin, coriander,

caraway, cardamon, and fenugreek, take two ounces
and a half each of cumin and coriander seeds, one and
a half ounce each of caraway and cardamon seeds, and
one half ounce of fenugreek, and roast them together
in a clean frying pan over a slow fire, with diligent
stirring. Grind the hot seeds, and mix the hot powder
thoroughly with the turmeric mixture. This modification of the process serves to give the currie a much
more mellow flavour. When the currie powder has
cooled, put it into well corked small glass bottles.
Ahmuty's Chutnee is one of the most delicious condiments to be eaten with curries.

Over indulgence in condiments should be carefully
avoided, as it is certainly injurious to health. Dr.
Edward Smith, in his classical book on foods, truly
observes that "the use of currie is less necessary and
defeasible in a temperate than in a hot climate, and it
is rare for one in England to tolerate the quantity of
capsicum which is relished in India." I have been
occasionally invited in England to partake of curries
hotter than the hottest Indian, yet which my Amphy-
trions would not scruple to call mild as mother's milk.
A very little of such a condiment will go a very long
way. Mustard and pepper, which are excellent condiments in their way, are also but too frequently
used in large quantities that can rationally only be
expected to injuriously irritate the stomach, instead of

simply stimulating it gently. Upon one point, at least, there cannot I think be too opinions, to wit, that children's food ought to be kept free from high spices and seasonings.

II.

SALADS.

I HAVE here, at the outset, to state my uncompromising rejection of the almost universal practice of washing green salads to prepare them for the bowl. The grand old cook, from whom I learnt in the days of my childhood, would never allow a drop of water to come near a salad leaf. She preferred wiping her green salads quite clean with a cloth, leaf by leaf, which is not much more labour, after all, than having to wash and drain the salad. But there is really no need to wipe every leaf. The very dirty outside leaves ought to be rejected altogether. They are only fit for fuel, and are certainly not worth the dressing that would have to be lavished on them. After heavy rains, salad may advantageously be rinsed with the watering pot whilst in the ground. The rays of the sun may safely be left to take off the water. The salad should then

be pulled when wanted. If it is wished to keep the
salad fresh the root should be stuck into moist sand in
the cellar. The firm heads of lettuce barely ever
harbour grit, or flies, or slugs within their folds, still
they ought to be pulled asunder, and carefully examined
and wiped if necessary. Leaves with much grit or
mould on them, or invaded by flies, slugs or insects
should be thrown away, at least the part affected. Perfectly dry fresh leaves will take kindly to the oil in the
dressing, washed leaves much less so. The water on the
washed leaves of course cannot but reduce the strength
of the vinegar, and as it is necessarily an indeterminate
quantity, it puts you out in your reckoning.

All green salads are the better for being kept a few
hours in the cellar before being prepared for the bowl.
Never put knife to your green salad, except just to
remove the lower part of the stalk. Pull and pluck the
leaves to suitable pieces with your fingers; the touch
of the knife tends to injure the delicacay of the salad,
more particularly its appearance when mixed in the
bowl.

The substitution of wiping for washing is not such a
very unheard of innovation as it may look to many.
Many friends in Germany and England have taken to
it on my strong recommendation—nay, even in France,
where they are wonderfully conservative in culinary
matters.

The old French salad dressing contained only three ingredients—oil, vinegar, and salt—to wit.

They had a saying in France, in the olden times, that it took four to make a good dressing and mix the salad well. A spendthrift for the oil, a miser for the vinegar, a sage for the salt, and a madman to mix. In those days the salt was sprinkled over the leaves in the bowl, the vinegar and the oil poured on, and the mixing done by vigorously stirring the mess in the bowl with a wooden or horn spoon and fork, or with two forks. It would be nearer the mark to substitute furiously for vigorously. I have occasionally seen a French salad mixer jump about like one possessed, madly driving at the tender salad leaves with his implements, as if he had to avenge a personal injury upon them.* Tarragon was mostly added, mint and chervil, &c., by way of seasoning; also shalots or onions finely chopped, or a few shaves from a clove of garlic; slices of beetroot, a thin slice or two of boiled celery root; a dash of black pepper; one or two teaspoonfuls of Bordeaux or Dijon mustard; cream or milk; sugar; the yolk of an egg, raw or hard boiled, and pounded fine—nay, even anchovy paste !†

---

* We dispense with the services of the madman now, as the dressing is mixed separately, and we mix our salads as lightly as practicable, which makes them look all the fresher and more appetising.

† To add anchovy paste to a green salad dressing seems more

I, for my part, prefer my salad dressing made simply
with oil, vinegar, salt, a sprinkling of pepper, a little
tarragon, mint and chervil for seasoning, a dash of
Worcester or Harvey, and a drop or two of garlic
vinegar. I am rather careful with the salt, as nothing
is easier than to oversalt a salad. Also, I do not hold
with the notion that it takes three parts of oil to one
of vinegar. As a rule, I find three oil to two vinegar
amply sufficient. The best Lucca oil only should be
used, and the best French vinegar (proof strength of
five per cent. pure acetic acid, sp. gr. of 1·019). Hard-
boiled eggs, anchovies as per foot note, slices of beet,
finely chopped onions or shalots (moistened with vinegar,
which gives them a nice colour), may be placed on the
table in small plates or dishes, to be added to the salad
according to taste.

If you have no garlic vinegar at hand, you may give
just the faintest suspicion of garlic, such as cannot
possibly incommode or offend the most fastidious, by
rubbing a cut clove of garlic on the soft side of a bread

---

than absurd. Yet have I seen it done over and over again. But
a few anchovies *are* an improvement. Only, they should be properly prepared. Wash your anchovies repeatedly and thoroughly
in cold water, place them in a stone or glass jar with the best
French vinegar, and let them stand a few days before using them.
By this time the bones are quite soft, so it matters not whether
you take them out or leave them. Cut your anchovies—one per
person—up very small, and add them to the salad dressing.

crust, placing this in a large wooden salad spoon at the
bottom of the bowl, pouring either oil or vinegar over
it, and letting it stand some fifteen minutes, then
removing the crust, and mixing the oil or vinegar in
the spoon with the other ingredients.

Salad dressing should be made and mixed a few
hours before it is required for the salad.

There is really no absolute need of yolk of egg to
blend the oil and vinegar together. Beating the two
liquids and the salt with a spoon will suffice to blend
them to a smooth cream.

In Germany a peeled soft boiled potato or two,
crushed to a mash with a spoon, is often used as an
economical substitute for yolk of egg, and I have been
unblushingly told it is nearly the same thing—if not
even better; but I do not believe it; a mashed potato
has nothing of the yolk of egg about it.

Most green salads are delicate and tender, and easily
broken or injured by clumsy mixing. Two wooden forks
should be used, and the leaves should never be pushed
down, or poked at, or stirred round in the bowl, but
only gently lifted and turned with the forks. Some
people have a notion that the oil should be used
separately from the dressing, the salad being first
lightly mixed with the oil, then carefully turned in the
dressing. They say it makes the salad more tender. I
must confess I have never found it so; that is to say,

of course, where the oil and vinegar are carefully blended. The garnishing and ornamentation of a salad in the bowl is entirely a matter of taste. All green salads should be fresh made, and eaten fresh.

A large bowl to mix the salad in is always a great desideratum. Nothing tends more to incomplete mixing than a bowl which is not large enough for the salad.

The following is a German recipe how to prepare a delicate and elegant LOBSTER SALAD: Take one or several good-sized hen lobsters ready boiled, pick out the flesh of the body and great claws, cut it into longish slices or slips, and lay them in a salad bowl. Chop shalots, parsley and tarragon very fine (quantities according to requirement)—say three ounces of shalots and one ounce each of parsley and tarragon to each lobster—add pepper, salt, oil, and vinegar in proper proportions as required, with a wineglassful of hock or chablis, and mix with a couple of hard-boiled yolks of eggs. Pour this dressing over the lobster in the bowl. Garnish with two or three hard-boiled eggs cut into disks, or into eighths, a few anchovies boned and rolled up, the coral of the lobsters, and an ounce of capers, and border with small rounds of toast with caviar.

To make a nice and digestible MIXED LOBSTER AND GREEN SALAD, take a good-sized boiled hen lobster, pick out the flesh of the body and great claws, and cut it

into longish slips, mix a tinned Rock Bay lobster lightly
with this, so as not to spoil the look of either. Then
pull the leaves of a head of lettuce and an endive
asunder into small pieces, and mix this also lightly with
the lobster. Take the same dressing as in the preceding
recipe, and pour it over the lobster and the green salad
in the bowl. Mix lightly with two wooden forks.
Garnish with hard-boiled eggs cut across in eighths, slices
of pickled cucumber, beetroot, the coral of the lobster,
an ounce of capers, four or five anchovies boned and
cut into fourths, and a few delicate celery and endive
leaves between. You may omit either the fresh or the
tinned lobster, for greater economy or for greater
delicacy.

The CUCUMBER has had a long and hard fight to
gain and maintain undisputed admittance among
"salad plants." For a long time the medical profession,
at least many of its leading professors, frowned upon
the harmless vegetable. Thus, it is related that the
famous Abernethy would often give consultants a
recipe for preparing a good cucumber salad, and tack to
it, by way of rider, his stern advice to fling the dish,
when made, out of the window, for even should it
alight on the head of some passer-by, he would add, it
would do less harm than if it were eaten—which,
simply, was the rankest nonsense.

I remember about half-a-century ago, when I was in

the Jardin du Dey hospital, in Algiers, that whenever
in the cucumber season a patient was admitted to our
division, suffering from stomachic or enteric disorder,
my *chef,* Surgeon-major Antonini, would, without further
preamble, come down upon the unlucky man with the
stereotyped stern apostrophe: "*Malheureux! vous avez
mangé des concombres.*" And when the patient, as
was mostly the case, would disclaim the impeachment;
he would add, with a grunt of relief, "*Ah! vous n'en
avez pas mangé: tant mieux pour vous: alors vous
pourrez vous en tirer.*"

Another of my illustrious chiefs, M. Des Guidi, the
famous homœopathist of Lyons, held the innocent
cucumber in holy abhorrence, more particularly eaten
with salt, oil, and vinegar. Upon this subject we were
often at fierce war, for I have always been passionately
fond of the noble vegetable. We had among our consultants a M. Dolfus, an Alsatian by birth, who fully
shared my affection for cucumbers. He suffered from
periodical seizures of gout, which M. Des Guidi would
invariably and exclusively attribute to cucumber salad.
Well, poor Dolfus was knocked down one day in the
Cours d'Herbouville by a runaway horse; the hind hoofs
struck him on the head, and he died on the spot. A
gentleman, who had seen the accident, brought us the
sad intelligence. "Ah!" cried he, "poor Dolfus is
gone." Before he could utter another syllable, M. Des

Guidi broke in, " Gone !" cried he, " Well, well, I
always told him those cursed cucumbers would be the
death of him !" The gentleman stared, and proceeded
to explain that it was a horse and not a dish of
cucumbers that had killed poor Dolfus. " Well," said
the obstinate theorist, not a whit abashed, " had it not
been for the accident he would surely have died of
cucumber !" Deceased was in his eighty-second year,
and had all his life indulged in this favourite delicacy
of his, without—as he often told me—ever having
suffered the least inconvenience from it.

Even now that the old prejudice of the profession
against cucumber salad has given way a little, the least
rumour of cholera or cholerina even suffices to revive it
in full vigour, and the old prohibition is applied again to
it and its fellow sufferer on such occasions, the delicious
cherry, the ever to be remembered glorious gift of
Lucullus to Europe, which constitutes his chiefest claim
to a pre-eminent place in the Pantheon of benefactors
of man. And anent this, I cannot resist the temptation
to tell a bright little legend, which I dearly love to
believe rests on a sound historic foundation. About
two centuries ago, that high-heeled, low-souled Bourbon,
Louis XIV., sent his ruffian bands into the Palatinate,
with his own and his truculent minister, Louvois',
ruthless orders, to lay waste and utterly destroy that
flourishing part of Germany. The devilish deed was

done. Upon the ultimate withdrawal of the murderers and incendiaries from the wasted land, hundreds of stragglers fell victims to the wild justice of revenge executed upon them by the unhappy peasants, driven to despair by the destruction of their crops, the burning of their homes. There were noble exceptions, however. Among others, a sorely wounded French soldier had his life spared and saved by a good German, in whose bosom even the darkness of despair had not been able to quench the divine glow of mercy and charity. The grateful Frenchman, it is said, repaid his rescuer's goodness many thousandfold, by bringing a number of young cherry trees from France, to plant them on the land of the man who had saved and sheltered him.

To return to our present theme, the cucumber. It must be conceded that the old popular way of eating cucumbers in lumps, with or without the skin, half drowned in sharp vinegar, with a very considerable dash of pepper, might not be the most wholesome. Some forty years ago I used to see it placed on the table with salmon, without a drop of oil. I have also, but too often—even within the last ten years—had occasion to remonstrate against the irrational method of sprinkling salt over the sliced cucumber, and draining off the fluid drawn by the salt. This strange proceeding, which, I am sorry to say, is not yet entirely a thing of the past, is based upon an

erroneous notion that it is in this fluid that the
assumed unwholesome property of the cucumber
resides. I have even seen the water squeezed out,
which, of course, leaves barely aught behind but tough
woody fibre. Some believe that cucumber salad requires
a larger proportion of vinegar than oil. This also
seems, to me, based on a wrong notion.

I think I can recommend the following recipe:—
Cut off about an inch and a half of the thin end of the
cucumber,and try whether there is bitterness in the piece
cut off. If there is, an additional slice or two must be
removed, until the part last removed is free from
bitterness. If you commence at once, without this
precaution, to pare the cucumber, the knife will carry
the bitterness along with it, even down to the thick
end. You should always pare your cucumber in the
direction of from the thick to the thin end. If you
happen to get hold of a cucumber abounding with
seeds, you may remove these, and slice only the pulp.
I always leave the seeds in, the same as I do in tomatos.
This is merely a matter of opinion. When your
cucumber is duly pared, slice it as fine as practicable.
A cucumber cutter or slicer will answer the purpose
best. In Germany they have excellent slicers, consisting of five or six sharp blades, successively superposed
on one another, and set in a suitable frame. Sprinkle
pepper over the sliced cucumber, which may, without

disadvantage, be kept an hour or two before dressing.
The dressing consists of oil and vinegar in the usual
proportions, with pepper and salt and finely chopped
tarragon, also a drop or two of garlic vinegar, the whole
intimately mixed. Into this dressing the cucumber
slices are put, and turned lightly with a wooden salad
spoon and fork, or two wooden forks. The salad should
be served at once and eaten fresh, though à la rigueur
a portion of it may be kept overnight. Shalots or
onions cut into small cubic pieces, and moistened with
vinegar, may be served with the salad. Some advise
that the sliced cucumber should first be dressed simply
with the oil, then with the vinegar, &c. I have tried
both ways, and I have not found the least noticeable
difference. This, again, is a matter of opinion and
taste. The addition of tomatos improves the delicacy
of a cucumber salad, and incontestably aids the digestion of the article, as anyone may easily find by dressing
part of the salad with tomatos, another without, and
keeping the two till next morning, when it will be
found that the part with the tomatos is converted into
a loose pulp, whereas the other part remains nearly unaltered.

There are a variety of other salads, made with
herrings, anchovies, potatoes, white summer cabbage,
beans, cauliflowers, sourcrout, beetroot, celery, &c. ; cold
roast meat, fish, various scraps, &c., &c. I can only

o

touch on a few of them. However, the dressing is
pretty nearly the same for all.

HERRING SALAD may be made in the simplest way
as follows :—Take six salted Dutch herrings, which
you may easily procure at a German provision shop.
Gut, skin, and wash them, and lay them three or four
hours in cold water. Bone them, and cut them into
small pieces. Have at least two soft roes among them,
mix these with the quantity of vinegar required for the
salad, and work the mixture through a tamis. Add the
proper proportion of oil, ground pepper, and a glass of
Burgundy or Bordeaux wine. Boil a pound of Dutch
salad potatoes in the skin, peel them and cut them
into slices while hot. If the slices seem too large, cut
every one of them in four. Chop four ounces of
shalots very fine, with one ounce each of tarragon and
capers. Pare six sour apples, and cut them into small
cubic pieces, removing the core, &c. Mix all these
ingredients together with the herrings in a bowl, and
pour the dressing over them. Stir thoroughly with a
wooden spoon and fork.

Some lay the herrings from six to eight hours in
milk, which certainly makes them more mellow. A
pound of roast veal cut into small cubic pieces is often
added along with the potatoes, or two pounds in lieu of
them. Also a few anchovies, up to half-a-dozen, and
lampreys cut into pieces about an inch long. Preserved

ginger, shredded fine, is also sometimes added ; so is beetroot and pickled cucumber. This salad improves vastly by keeping over-night.

A so-called RUSSIAN SALAD is made simply with sourcrout fresh from the cask, squeezed pretty dry, and mixed with a common salad dressing. The Russians are fond of this—I cannot say I am.

In the year of the first great Exhibition, I became intimately acquainted with one of the chief actors and factors in the Vienna rising of 1848—Dr. Karl Tausenau, a gentleman of the highest attainments—a born orator, an accomplished linguist, one of the best and soundest classical scholars of our time, no mean Orientalist, a fluent, accentless speaker of seven European languages, including Czech and Magyar, a profound historian, a really good rational physician, and last, though certainly not least, a mighty Cook. In those days, I was still a busy dabbler in revolutionary politics, so there were several bonds of union between us, and it did not take us long to become fast friends. Tausenau was President of the Agitation Union, the Secretaryship of which was conferred upon me. We conspired and worked in sweet harmony of aspirations and taste. Tausenau expected the advent in London, on a short visit, of one of the most promising factors in the European Upheaval which we were then meditating, a Polish gentleman who went by the name of Bosak, but whose real name

was Haucke, the son of the last Minister of War of the
Kingdom of Poland, Voivode Haucke. His sister—
now Princess of Battenberg—married soon after Prince
Alexander of Hesse.

Tausenau, desirous of celebrating Bosak's advent
among us, gave a grand spread to a select few at his
chambers in Barnard's Inn, Holborn. There were six
of us gathered there—Tausenau, Frank, Fickler (of
Constance), Arnold Ruge, my own humble self, and the
Guest of the evening. It was a wondrous spread.
Among the dishes figured a huge bowl of POLISH
SALAD, in special honour of Bosak.

That salad was of my making and mixing. The ingredients were :—Three pounds of roast fillet of veal,
two pounds and a half of roast beef, and two pounds of
roast pork; four heads of Neapolitan lettuce, and one
beetroot, sliced ; six anchovies, boned and chopped fine,
with six ounces of shalots, two ounces each of tarragon
and capers, and one ounce of parsley. For the dressing,
I used sixteen salad spoonfuls of oil to eight of vinegar,
a tablespoonful of salt, and an ounce of ground pepper
and pimento, mixed ; also a tablespoonful of mustard, of
my own making, and eight soft-boiled eggs. Bosak's
eyes seemed to dwell with delight upon this national
dish ; yet was there a shade of melancholy regret in
them. "A pity," he murmured, "that there are only six
of us to eat it, when there are so many unhappy exiles

going about with empty stomachs." "*Six* of us!" cried
Frank; "six, indeed! Why, we are *eighteen* here to
eat it—four of us others, six of Fickler, and eight of
Tausenau!" The insinuation was vilely exaggerated,
but there was a substantial substratum of truth in it.
Every man, however great, has his foibles. Tausenau
worshipped his stomach. A Lucullus and an Apicius
rolled into one could barely have given an adequate
notion of his intense gastrolatry. Joseph Fickler of
Constance was very much similarly disposed; and both
might reasonably be counted for several at a dinner
table with good things on it. Alas! alas! They are
all but myself gone long since to the mysterious beyond
where we may hope to find the grosser part of our poor
humanity stripped off—Tausenau, Fickler, Frank, and
Ruge—and Bosak, who fell fighting under Garibaldi in
the Franco-German War of 1870—1871.

III.

UNFERMENTED BEVERAGES—COFFEE—TEA—CHOCOLATE.

A.—COFFEE.

"Coffee as in France," is the alluring announcement
seen even nowadays not unfrequently in the windows
of coffee-houses, &c. The inviting promise thus held
out to the lover of a genuine cup of coffee is based, of

course, upon the assumption that France is specially and exceptionally the land where they understand the art of making coffee better than in any other part of the world, more particularly in England, that "know nuffink" Topsy of countries—to listen to English self-depreciation. Sterne's slightly unwarranted conceit about their ordering many things so much better in bright clever France than in our own dull stupid land, has been parroted so often that many people in this country have come to believe in it as an article of faith. Now the truth of the matter is that there are really not so very many things that they order better in France— and the French themselves are quite aware of that fact.

I once read of an Englishman of the true Sterne type who, returning from a trip to France in the olden days when visits to the Contintent were rather rare occurrences, expressed his astonishment at the advanced state of education in France, as he had heard even the little children in the street speak French. Leaving the ludicrous side of the story out of the question, it might, indeed, be remarked that little children in France do speak French—but after a fashion; as we have it upon the unimpeachable authority of the great Balzac that the beautiful French language is but little known in France.* So we may perhaps be permitted to express

---

* "Cette belle langue française, si peu connue en France," says that eminent writer.

a diffident doubt whether the art of making coffee to perfection is actually quite so perfectly and universally understood in France as it is popularly supposed to be.

Do not let me be misunderstood here. Not for an instant would I venture to deny but that there are to be found all over France many *cafés*, the proprietors or managers of which really understand how to make good coffee, and where the demand for the article is so brisk and constant that it is easy to make and supply it fresh and fresh, which leaves no time for it to be spoiled by having to be kept hot a longer or shorter time after making. I also admit that most excellent coffee is to be got in many private houses in France. But such are the exceptions from the rule; and these are to be found as numerous in many other countries besides France, and, I make bold to say, more especially in England.

I have in my time travelled much about in France, traversing that country in many directions, and I must say that I have but too often had a stale decoction of burnt coffee and chicory placed before me, in lieu of a fresh, full-flavoured, and fragrant infusion of genuine properly made coffee, such as, on the other hand, I have found in England at least as frequently as anywhere else.

The fact is coffee making is an art, and it seems to me at least fairly open to doubt whether this art is exceptionally well understood in France. There is the

important branch of mixing and blending several kinds
of beans together so as to combine body and fragrance.
I do not think French coffee dealers and coffee makers
care very much to cultivate and practise that branch;
and when they do, I have my doubts whether sufficient
care is taken by them to bring the different beans to be
blended to the same degree of dryness before proceeding
to mix and roast them. The natural result is that one
class of beans may only just be reaching the stage of
light-yellowishness when the other classes may actually
have passed through the umber-brown to the black stage
of torrefaction, and may be burning to cinders. The
proper sizing of the beans, again, is but rarely attended
to: a small bean may be burnt to coal by the time a
large one is only just properly roasting. These are important points, which are but too often ignored and
neglected in France just as much as elsewhere.

It is in the process of roasting that the volatile
aromatic oil to which coffee owes its fragrance is
generated or evolved. The generation of the oil com-
mences when the beans are roasted to a yellowish-
brown colour; it is completed when the beans are
assuming a chestnut-brown tint. Continued roasting
beyond this point can only lead to the destruction of
the oil generated in the earlier stages of the process.
When the beans are burnt to blackness the oil has
completely passed off—and unfortunately, in France

an1 other parts of the Continent, coffee is but too often roasted black. Besides, many roasters think the addition of a small lump of butter, nay, even of an onion, a desirable improvement. Why not a clove of garlic. or two, which would be just as rational. By the side of such vagaries even the adulteration of coffee with chicory, &c., looks almost less hurtful. And, to crown all, I am credibly informed some of these wonderful coffee makers and improvers in certain parts of France and Germany have of late taken to a new refinement. They wash the coffee before roasting it. Yes, *ni plus ni moins*, as the French say: they put the raw beans on a colander, and pour cold water over them. Then they rub the wetted beans in a cloth, and try to dry them again in the sun or in an oven; or they simply put them into the roaster wet as they come from the rubbing cloth! All who know that the drying of the bean is one of the most important processes on coffee plantations, and how the least indication of a coming shower is apt to fill the planter's soul with dismay, lest it should come down upon his precious drying beans, depreciating their value, must be at a loss to fix upon an intelligible reason or motive for this strange proceeding. Well these bean washers assert as their chief reason that the beans may be artificially coloured, forsooth, and the water will take the false coloring off!

To have your coffee pure and well-flavoured, and of proper strength, you should always purchase it in the green bean of a well-reputed firm. The best coffees to buy are Mysore and Mocha, Java and Jamaica Mountain, Old Turkey and Costa Rica—and, good Ceylon, which will serve excellently well for blending. I think it can be got in the green bean at something like 10d. a pound by the quarter cwt., which is a consideration.

The choice of one sort or another is a matter of taste. I prefer Mocha, Java, Jamaica Mountain and Ceylon, always blending them in the proportion of six parts of Mocha to five each of Java and Jamaica; or seven of Mocha to five of Java and four of finest Ceylon; or five parts each of Mocha and Java to three parts each of Jamaica and Ceylon. 1 like the three mixtures equally well.

Pick your beans carefully, and size each sort separately. Genuine Old Mocha is perfectly dry, the other sorts are moist, as a rule, and require, accordingly, a little preliminary heating to bring them up to the same degree of dryness. As you have to do of course only with small quantities at a time, this may be readily done on porcelain dishes set on the hot-plate or put in the oven. Ten to fifteen or twenty minutes will generally suffice. Then mix the several sizes of the several sorts—the small, the medium sized, and the large—and proceed to roast one of the sizes, no matter which, putting the two others by in well-stoppered glass bottles.

Never roast more than you actually require for immediate use, and let your coffee go instantly from the roaster to the mill, from the mill to the biggin or the Cafetière. It cannot be too often and too earnestly urged that the oil to which the coffee owes its wondrous fragrance is volatile, and that its dissipation and diffusion through the surrounding air begins from the very instant of its full generation. The beans may be roasted in a small iron cylinder, with a sliding door in it, through which the raw coffee is put in. The cylinder is turned slowly round over a pretty brisk, though not over-fierce charcoal, coal or gas fire—so that all the beans in it may in time be exposed to the same heat. The proper speed of the cylinder is from nine to fifteen revolutions per minute. My friend Tausenau, who was an accomplished coffee maker, would put the beans into the heated cylinder, and keep turning for twelve minutes, giving the cylinder an occasional shake. By this time the beans would be yellowish-brown; he would then take the cylinder off the fire, and shake it continuously for several minutes, which just sufficed to deepen the light brown colour to umber. It takes me, as a rule, about fifteen or sixteen minutes to roast my beans equally to chestnut brown. I am guided in a great measure by the bursting and crackling of the silver skin and the fragrant smell of the roasting coffee, as the process is nearing completion. I have often roasted coffee in an enamelled frying-pan in the absence of a cylinder, which is an easy operation enough. You must simply take care to put only a thin layer of beans in the pan, and to keep stirring with a glass rod. I never, on any account, roast my coffee beyond chestnut-brown—rather light than otherwise—and I transfer it at once from the roaster to the mill. For very small quantities, say an ounce or so for my own personal drinking, I prefer the pan to the cylinder, as I am better able to watch the bursting and scattering of the silver skin. If you use an enamelled frying-pan for roasting your coffee, on no account whatever use it for any other purpose, as there is barely a smell that coffee will not attract and acquire to the impairment of its fragrance.

I am told that Mr. William Sugg has lately invented a self-acting coffee-roasting apparatus. I have had no occasion yet to try this new invention, so cannot speak from personal experience of it's working. But from the description given to me I am inclined to say that it seems practicable and practical.

Coffee loses in roasting from twelve to twenty-four per cent., according to the degree of roasting given, which is indicated by the several shades of colour through which the bean passes, to wit, yellowish-brown, chestnut-brown, and deep brown or black. The last

gradation I reject altogether, as the aroma passes off
from the instant the chestnut-brown is reached. It is
the strongest objection I have to the continental
practice. In my own roasting I even stop short of the
pronounced chestnut-brown. My beans lose eighteen
per cent.—Tausenau's practice stops at sixteen per cent.
loss.

Adapt the size of your cylinder to the quantity of
coffee you have to roast at a time; I need hardly add
that there should always be sufficient room left for the
beans to swell and move freely about.

Grinding is another important element in the preparation of good coffee. The finer the mill grinds, the
stronger is the infusion, and accordingly the more
economical the process. Coarse-ground beans will
yield only eighty per cent., nay, as low as sixty-five or
sixty per cent. of infusion of the same strength as fine-
ground beans will produce. In the East they generally
pound the fresh-roasted beans in a marble mortar with a
wooden pestle to a fine powder. Brillat Savarin
found by actual experiment that the pounded coffee
gave a superior liquid to that produced from the
ground coffee. However, grinding is more expeditious,
and with a fine mill the result is almost equally satisfactory.

Always pass your beans fresh and hot from the
roaster to the mill, and grind without delay.

Infusing the ground or pounded coffee is certainly
not the least important element in the preparation of
good coffee. It is at this critical stage that most of our
coffee is spoiled, yet the proper process is simplicity itself.

There are two distinct ends to be attained by the
operation, to wit, to extract from the ground or pounded
beans the greatest amount of body and fragrance, and
to obtain a clear limpid fluid. The former end is by far
the more important of the two, though it is, of course,
most desirable that the other end should be equally
attained, if practicable. As Mr. Tegetmeier expresses it
with admirable brevity and clearness, " The flavour of
coffee depends upon a volatile substance which is driven
off by boiling; to preserve its taste, it should therefore
be made without boiling,"—in other words, coffee should
be an infusion, not a decoction.

Yet, strange to say, there are many people who will
insist upon boiling their coffee, and wonder, forsooth,
that it should have no fragrance! In fact, it would
seem to be deemed by many of much higher importance
that their coffee should be a transparently clear fluid
than that it should be good coffee in the proper sense
of the word.

The following recipe is copied literally from a high
French authority:—" Put two ounces of fresh ground
coffee of the best quality into a coffee pot, and pour
eight coffee cups of boiling water on it; *let it boil six*

minutes, pour out a cupful two or three times, and return it again; then put two or three isinglass chips into it, and pour one large spoonful of boiling water on it; *boil it five minutes more*, and set the pot by the fire to keep hot for ten minutes, and you will have coffee of a beautiful clearnes." True, the fluid may be beautifully clear, but it certainly can no longer be called coffee by any stretch of the imagination.

There are several ways of obtaining a genuine bright infusion of fragrant coffee. One of these is the Eastern way, minus the pounding—that is to say, put about three teaspoonfuls of fresh-roasted and fresh-ground coffee hot from the mill into a large breakfast-cup (half a pint) and fill up with boiling water close to the brim. Stir the mixture well, and let it stand a minute or two; then put in a tablespoonful of cold water, which will make the grounds at once subside to the bottom.

There are also several hydraulic coffee pots, in which the boiling water is drawn through the ground coffee, with a view to obtain a bright infusion.

Then there is Ash's apparatus which by means of a jacket filled with boiling water keeps up the temperature, producing thus a strong infusion.

The French coffee pot, made of two cylindrical vessels, the upper with a strainer in which the coffee powder is placed, and through which the clear infusion runs into the lower one, is very practical, particularly

with a double disk of muslin placed in the strainer
before putting the ground coffee in, which almost serves
the purpose of a perfect filter. I incline much to this
French coffee pot, as it is both expeditious and
economical—which the so-called Vesuvian and Venetian
hydraulic apparatus certainly are not.

Our old cook used to make her coffee in an earthen
biggin, into which she suspended a funnel-shaped
muslin bag sewn all round to a silver ring at the top
with hooks to catch hold of the rim of the biggin. The
boiling water was poured over this, and left two
minutes or three, to extract the coffee in the bag, which
was then withdrawn. The coffee was always most
fragrant and of amber brightness. This will be found
an excellent way for small quantities, not above two
ounces at the most.

I have also in the course of my life tasted many
excellent cups of coffee made by simply immersing for
the short space of three or four minutes a sock with the
fresh roasted and ground coffee powder in it, in the
requisite quantity of boiling water in a suitable vessel
set on the hot plate to keep the temperature up to the
proper degree during the immersion. The socks used
for the purpose should be quite new from the shop, and
should, moreover, be boiled for half an hour in clean
soft water to remove the least trace of extraneous
matter of any kind. This may seem slightly finical;

but there are possible associations of ideas which had better be kept out of the range of suggestive specu‌lation.

There is a story told of an English Officer's Irish servant, rather a handy fellow, with some small spice of Lover's Andy in him. His master had invited some brother officers, and Mickey was instructed to make the after-dinner coffee. " Boil one of my new Balbriggans," said the master, " and use it for making the coffee." Well, in due time the coffee was served. It was found delicious, and it was hinted that another cup would be acceptable. " Yes," said the gratified host, " it is a simple way of making really good coffee; only it is not economical. A sock will only do for three or four times at the most, as the bitter taste of the extract will become more and more prominent each time the sock is used—and Balbriggans are three shillings a pair." " Arrah, thin, your honour," here Mickey broke in unexpectedly, " I thot that same, so I tuk one of yer honour's ould wans, which was clane."

The coffee was first-rate, no doubt, but somehow or other the guests did not want that other cup at the time.

Seamless socks, which can be bought at 2d. or 2½d. the pair, will answer equally well as Balbriggan. I need hardly remark that, as the boiling water has to gain free access to every grain of the powder to extract the essence from it within the limited space of a few minutes, this process will do well only for smaller quantities of ground coffee, up to three or four ounces at the most, sufficient for a dozen small cups or *demi-tasses* of black coffee—to be served with cognac after dinner. A few lumps of sugar should be put in to sweeten the cup, and a small glass of cognac carefully spread over the surface of the coffee and set fire to, a lump of sugar with a dash of cognac over it in a teaspoon to be held *into* the flame (not *over* it, which would simply blacken the spoon). The result is simply delicious. For breakfast, or milk-coffee in general, pour out a small cup into a half-pint cup, and fill up with *boiling hot* milk. I have a notion that the addition of sugar has a tendency to impair the full fragrance of the coffee. This, however, is after all simply a matter of taste. Some prefer cream to their coffee, others take preserved Swiss milk. Coffee epicures take the infusion neat. The proper proportion of water to be used depends, of course, upon the strength of the infusion desired. Two ounces of ground coffee will make one pint of essence of coffee, one pint and a half and a little more of very excellent strong coffee. A quarter of a pound is amply sufficient then to give coffee infusion for twelve or fourteen breakfast cups of *Café au lait*—so that the actual price of a large breakfast cup of splendid milk-coffee, which it would not be easy to match anywhere on the Continent, will not exceed 1¼d., including cost of coffee, milk, sugar, fuel, labour, interest on cost of apparatus, wear and tear of same, &c., &c. Another precious rule is to drink your coffee fresh made. Make always only just sufficient for your actual requirement—and not even a quarter of a cup beyond. It is one of the greatest defects in coffee-houses, here as well as on the Continent, that they make their coffee in larger quantities than required, as a rule, for immediate use, and have accordingly to keep a larger or smaller portion of it hot for customers expected to drop in. Coffee made to perfection cannot be kept hot even for a few minutes without the aroma taking flight.

I remember, more especially, how, in 1867, when the coffee at the Place de la Tour St. Jacques, which at that time enjoyed my special patronage, was made in strict accordance with the rules, I would occasionally get a cup of exquisite coffee there, and would engage any friend, whom I happened to meet after, to go to the Café and have a cup of the delicious beverage, forgetful of the time it would take them to reach the place. No wonder they marvelled at my warm recommendation of a semi-bitter, semi-insipid hot liquid. I have in my mind devised what I believe to be a practicable apparatus to make single cups of fresh fragrant coffee separately, but simultaneously. A hint to enterprising capitalists in search of profitable investments. Hard water is said to make better coffee than soft water. I cannot speak positively upon the point, but I believe the fact to be so, as hard water, whilst fully extracting the volatile aromatic principle from the ground or powdered coffee, is not quite so well calculated as soft water in the comparatively short time of contact to extract equally the other, perhaps less desirable elements.

Always keep your coffee biggin or cafetière or other apparatus, &c., scrupulously clean for every fresh infusion—and heat them thoroughly with boiling water each time before use.

Strong coffee is, in my humble opinion, a better and safer stimulant than tea; it makes also a better food with boiling milk than the latter, and is accordingly more suitable for breakfast. A small cup—a *demi tasse* —neat, or with a modicum of cognac or *old* Jamaica rum, after dinner is certainly calculated to aid digestion. Quality not quantity should be the presiding rule in the use of coffee. Strong coffee taken *before* meals I hold to be injurious. Cold coffee diluted rather largely with milk and water is an excellent drink in summer and winter, and a much better and safer stimulant for the brain than alcoholic beverages. Young children should not have coffee given them nor, for the matter of that, tea either, whether green or black, strong or weak.

The only wholesome beverage in childhood is milk, neat or diluted more or less largely with good potable water. Strong black coffee is an excellent antidote in poisoning with opium, also in cases where strong tea, particularly green, has been indulged in to excess.

Excessive indulgence in strong coffee cannot but be injurious to health. One small cup mixed with an equal portion of boiling milk for breakfast, and one small cup after dinner, should not be exceeded.

B.—TEA.

The tea which I knew in the days of my childhood and youth was the Overland or Caravan Tea, imported from China into Siberia over Kiachta. GUNPOWDER and PEKOE were then the sorts chiefly used in Russia and Northern Germany. As this caravan tea had not been subjected to the action of the sea air, it retained its full aroma, and was—in my recollection at least—very superior in flavour and strength to any of even the choicest teas of the present time. But it was also extravagantly high-priced then, and simply an article of luxury, altogether beyond the reach of any but the well-to-do classes; and even by them it was used but sparingly. It was then generally flavoured with vanilla or canella.

I can even now vividly recall to mind our cook
making tea in those olden days. I think I see her now
before me with balance in hand, weighing small
quantities of black tea and green for mixing; for, with
her acute understanding, she knew that the two
differed very considerably in weight, bulk for bulk,
the compactly rolled green leaf weighing twice as much
as the loosely rolled black, and that two measures of
Pekoe were only equivalent to one of Gunpowder.
She infused her mixture in a close-covered earthen pot,
thoroughly heated first with boiling water, which was
poured off again before the tea mixture was put in.
She then put the pot in a deep stewpan, filled with
boiling water nearly up to the height of the immersed
pot, into which she proceeded to pour water in fierce
ebullition up to the brim. She then put the cover on,
and let her tea infuse exactly three minutes by the
kitchen clock, when she removed the teapot to the hob,
putting a woollen hood or cosey over it. Then she
would slowly turn, or rather dance, round nine times,
muttering strange words, which I at the time, with profound awe, took to be an incantation indispensable to
the success of the brew. I know now that this was
simply her way of timing herself. But in those days I
was delightfully innocent of the wicked and wily ways
of the world—and of the sex, and Thusnelda Irma's tea
incantation was something like an article of faith with

me; so much so, indeed, that when a few years later on I passed a vacation in Berlin with a schoolfellow, I one day surprised the lady of the house by artlessly telling her that I was afraid the tea she was making at the time would not turn out nice, as she had omitted the dance and the incantation! Well, well! I was then only rising thirteen, and so a fool's pardon was readily granted me. When the tea had thus been left to draw altogether some four to five minutes, cook transferred the contents of the pot to a Chinese teapot, heated previously with boiling water.

It seems that our best tea-makers are agreed now that four to five minutes' infusion will extract from tea all that it is desirable should be extracted.

Tea should always be made with soft water. The addition of soda to hard water to adapt it for tea making is, in my opinion, objectionable, as it must tend to destroy the respiratory action of the tea, and to impair its flavour. Distilled water and rain water, though the very perfection of *softness*, will not do for tea-making, as they contain neither air nor mineral ingredients. The Chinese take their water in preference from hill springs or running streams. Tea should always be made with water newly boiled, and boiled slowly rather than fast. The water should be actually bubbling when it is poured on the tea.

Tea is best with unboiled milk or cream.

Infusion of gunpowder or Hyson, unmixed with Pekoe, was in my time almost exclusively used for rum or arrack punch.

Tea is always best made in an earthen teapot, which should be kept scrupulously clean, and should be thoroughly dried inside each time after use, as a damp pot is apt to give a musty flavour to the infusion made in it.

I believe the delicate aroma of tea, especially of the finer sorts, is enjoyed best drunk from small cups of semi-strong infusions of high-class teas. The quantity of leaf used should not exceed sixty grains per cup; and I think one or two cups ought to do for a moderate tea-drinker. Professional tea-tasters use only about forty grains per cup. Good tea should not be flavoured with vanilla or canella—unless for green tea punch. I think fresh unboiled milk is preferable for tea to boiling milk. However, this is a matter of taste. For my own part, I like my tea best with lemon juice—and a dash of old Jamaica rum or arrack.

Strong tea is, in my humble opinion, decidedly objectionable. I have often seen as much as half an ounce, and more, of Souchong, or Congou, or Oulong, used to a single cup of tea. Drinking tea in quantities cannot but be hurtful to the constitution. We have it upon the unimpeachable authority of Mr. Tony Weller that at the ever memorable meeting of the Brick Lane

Branch of the United Grand Junction Ebenezer Temperance Association, some of the ladies were drowning themselves in tea, one disposing of no less than nine breakfast cups and a half, which made her "swell visibly" before Mr. Weller's eyes. But these were Temperance People, and it may reasonably be supposed that the beverage was *rather* weak. Still I cannot but think excessive indulgence in tea, strong or weak, must be hurtful to health.

Dr. Smith, in his great work on "Foods," says that excellent tea, both in body and aroma, may be prepared by simply putting the leaves into ordinary cold water, in a covered vessel, and keeping this over a gentle fire until the water boils, when the tea is ready for use. I have tried this plan, and have found it answer well, though I did not think at first it would. The most convenient way is to boil the water with the leaves in it by gas or a spirit-lamp on the table. Whilst I am finishing this paragraph, a lady tells me that one of the great rules in tea making is to calculate the quantity required to a nicety, and never to exceed that quantity. If your guests should wish for an additional cup or so, it is easy to make a fresh supply. This seems more rational, at all events, than the common way of pouring fresh relays of boiling water over the exhausted tea leaves in the pot, even with the addition of another spoonful or so of dry leaves.

C.—CHOCOLATE.

Chocolate ranks higher as a food than coffee and tea, as it contains a large proportion of fat and other nutritive elements. It also excites the nerves much less than either of the other two beverages, and makes a most agreeable food, especially boiled in milk, with the addition of an egg per cup.

It is a great pity that it should be so subject to adulteration, particularly with flour and starch. Even the sugar used in the manufacture of sweet chocolate becomes an element of sophistication when added beyond requirement—considering that the price of cocoa is at present more than three times that of sugar. Chocolate in powder is more especially liable to these frauds.

Get your chocolate at a well-reputed shop, and buy it in cakes or tablets, in preference to powder. Try to get the old unsweetened Spanish or Cophenhagen chocolate—hard as a rock; or, in default thereof, French or English tablets of the best-reputed makers. Unsweetened chocolate is always the best to use, and the cheapest, notwithstanding its apparently high price.

Chocolate may be made with water or with milk.

Scrape about a quarter of a pound of your unsweetened chocolate cake into a saucepan, and pour water on it only just barely sufficient to cover the chocolate. Set it on the fire, and stir with a wooden spoon until it forms a thickish paste. Sweeten to taste, and add a pint or a pint and a half of boiling water, more or less, according to the strength and quantity required, and boil for ten minutes, with diligent stirring. This is considered a very good way of making water chocolate.

For milk chocolate, which is prepared in the same way, a full quart of new milk should be used. Diluting this with one third part of water will rather improve the flavour of the chocolate than otherwise.

The following is my recipe to prepare a tasty and nutritious cup of chocolate:—Scrape a quarter of a pound of your unsweetened chocolate cake into a chocolate pot; add sugar to taste, with a cupful of new milk;* break six sound eggs into the pot, yolks and whites, and beat and blend the whole thoroughly. Then stir in a quart of boiling new milk. Or blend the chocolate and the well-beaten eggs thoroughly with half a pint of fresh milk and a tablespoonful of preserved milk, and stir in a quart of boiling water.

Chocolate should always be served fresh made.

The following is a good French recipe:—Boil equal

---

* This prevents the curdling of the egg upon the subsequent addition of the boiling milk. The same applies to egg-flip, &c., when a cupful of cold beer should be beaten up with the eggs, &c., before adding the hot beer.

quantities of good new milk and water. Scrape off
your chocolate cake what you require; take the milk
and water off the fire, throw in the chocolate, with sugar
to taste, and mix well and rapidly, so as to blend the
chocolate completely with the liquid. Serve with the
froth on.

IV.

FERMENTED DRINKS.

This most highly important branch of dietetics is so
vast and so far-extending in its aspects and bearings—
physiological, hygienic, moral, social, and political—that
it would be idle to attempt touching upon it, even
lightly, in a work of such limited scope as this.

Still there is a point intimately connected with the
subject upon which I crave permission to say a few
words. I am conscious that it may seem gratuitous on
my part, and unwarranted, yet I venture to make an
appeal to that tyrannical minority of earnest well-
meaning champions of abstinence who,. with the most
benevolent intention, would rob the poor man of his
beer, and strip life of much that enlivens it, cheering
and gladdening the heart of man, to be temperate in
their temperance, and to pause in their fierce crusade
against all things fermented. Why not wage war

instead upon that blackest plague-spot of the time—
the poisonous adulteration of our foods and drinks,
notably of good wholesome liquor? Then the sacred
cause of freedom would no longer be made to suffer
fatal injury from mistaken zeal, and the great and good
cause of true temperance would progress and prosper
all the more promptly and thoroughly for a little
tolerant forbearance extended to the rational enjoyment
of some of God's choicest gifts to man—jovial generous
wine and bonny beer, as the old song has it.*

Here I must stop, however reluctantly, winding up
simply with a few general directions and a small collection of recipes for compounding mixed drinks.

One of the most detrimental effects of alcohol upon
the human frame is that, owing to its strong affinity for
water, it abstracts that indispensable element from the
organs; and this effect can be mitigated only by
dilution.

No ardent spirits should therefore ever be taken

---

* The *rational* enjoyment, be it well understood, avoiding the
least approach to excess. *Children should on no account ever be
allowed to touch beer or wine.* Milk is their natural drink, and
good water, agreeably flavoured with fruit juices and syrups.
Unfortunately we but too often see how even the smaller children
of the poorer classes are made to imbibe beer and—much worse
and more perniciously detrimental to their health and well-being
—ardent spirits! which I, for one, cannot but indignantly hold
as a crime perpetrated upon the unhappy, helpless young
beings.

" *neat*," as it is termed, but always more or less largely
diluted with water, according to the actual strength of
the spirit, which depends upon the proportion of alcohol
in it. This proportion differs widely in the various
spirits—rums, brandies, whiskies, arracks, gins, &c.—
supplied by the trade. The legal standard strength is
fixed at 49·24 per cent. by weight of alcohol to 50·76
per cent. of water—which is very nearly half and half.
This is called proof. Spirits containing more water
than 50·76 per cent. are said to be under proof; when
they contain more alcohol than 49·24 per cent. by
weight they are over proof. By Act of Parliament
whisky, brandy, and rum are not to be sold weaker than
25° under proof, gin not weaker than 35° under proof,
which means that the former should always contain
39·4, the latter 36·5, per cent. by weight of alcohol.
There is much reason, however, to doubt that spirits of
the legal strength are always supplied by the retail
trade. Over proof, or even proof spirits, are, as a rule,
to be procured only wholesale. On the Continent, more
especially in Germany and Holland, but also in France,
I have often met with fine old rum of close upon 70
per cent. alcoholic strength. I am told that the old
navy rum supplied to the fleet contains 58 per cent.
by weight of absolute alcohol. I believe also that there
are many reputable firms in the United Kingdom that
sell good and genuine spirits of stated strength. The

best and safest way is always to deal with such firms; you need not then be afraid of having tricks of trade played upon you. An alcoholometer—which is an instrument for measuring the proportion of alcohol in a fluid—will be found most useful. It is inexpensive. The proportions given in the few recipes here subjoined are calculated upon proof strength; they have therefore to be increased or diminished according to the actual strength of the spirit at your disposal, the increase or decrease being added to or deducted from the quantity of water directed to be used.

Never use new spirits, but only the best old, ripened and mellowed by age, that have been kept in wood for many years. Here, again, dealing only with well-reputed firms will best safeguard you.

Even the weaker spirits sold should never be taken neat; they require still further dilution with water, to take the sting out of them, as it were, and to make them—with sugar, &c.—into harmless palatable and cheering toddy, grog, or punch. Everything is relative, of course, and no general rule can properly be laid down as to what the spirituous strength of a mixed drink should be. For my part, I think 125, and even 150 or 160 volumes of water added to old rum, &c., of proof strength may be held to be near the proper proportion for pretty good grog, toddy, or punch. I am sorry to say, however, that I have known people—not a few of

them, indeed—who would never put up with anything
short of proof, just with a dash of water in it, to persuade
themselves that they were not drinking it raw. Tastes
and inclinations differ, and it is never wise to be over
dogmatic.

If you use lemon or orange peel in your mixture,
pare the fruit as thin as practicable, cutting through the
minute cells contiguous to the surface, which hold the
essential oil, and carefully remove the portion of the
oil which adheres to the white pulp, by rubbing a lump
of sugar over it.

In mixing punches, grogs, or toddies in the bowl or
in the tumbler, always put in the sugar first, along with
the lemon peel and juice, then add water, cold or boiling, according to circumstances, in sufficient quantity to
melt the sugar; add the spirit to the solution, stir, and
add the rest of the water required. The simple reason
for this order of mixing is that the sugar dissolves much
more readily in water than in dilute spirit.

The quantity of sugar and lemon juice is entirely a
matter of taste. I use one ounce of lemon juice—a fine
lemon generally holds about two ounces of clear juice—
and two ounces of sugar per pint of water. I prefer
using a drop or two of essence of lemon or orange, &c.,
instead of peel. The result is more uniform.

The Rev. Deputy Shepherd Stiggins, though holding
all liquors as vanities, yet professedly disliked least the

liquor called Rum—with a squeeze of lemon, a slice of peel, and a lump or two of sugar in it. I forget now whether any mention was made of water; but I do not think there was.

Many years ago I was at a gathering of distinguished men of letters and artists in Regent Street. It was in Fraser's parlour. There were present, besides the proprietor of the establishment and of the then famous *Regina Magazine*, Dr. Maginn, Nimrod, Carlyle, the illustrious Michael Angelo Titmarsh, and several other pillars of Regina, more especially that noble Irish Corinthian, glorious Father Prout, who on this very occasion gave us his famous receipt for brewing a bowl "fit for the Gods on high Olympus, and the men then socially assembled in the Regina parlour," which he said differed from Schiller's equally famous receipt only in the unimportant omission of the aqueous element. "Every dhrop of wather you add spoils the punch," was the Father's authoritative dictum.

Well, the Rev. Stiggins might have been of the Father's faith in the "no water" tenet. If so, this is the only point on which I do not fully concur with him in his professed minimised dislike of the liquor called rum, which truly and admittedly is the least hurtful of ardent spirits, and the only one that has a well-founded claim to be mentioned among foods.

My favourite variety in the way of Punch is

Q

the IMPERIAL PINE APPLE PUNCH — when I can get it.

Slice a pine apple very thin—a West Indian pine will do. Peel four fine juicy oranges clean, removing every particle of the white pulp, and separate them into eighths. Put pine apple slices and oranges into a suitable bowl, along with twelve ounces of sugar, eight of lemon juice—(the juice of four fresh fine lemons)—and four or five drops each of essence of lemon, cinnamon, and vanilla. Add a quart of boiling water. Cover the bowl, and let it stand till quite cold. Then add to the contents a pint of old Jamaica rum, and half a pint of best arrack, a bottle of Hock and a wineglassful of green Chartreuse. Stir the mixture well with the ladle, and wind up by pouring in simultaneously a bottle of champagne and one of seltzer. Ladle out. Some prefer infusing about fifty grains each of canella and vanilla in the boiling water. I like the essences best. Natural seltzer in jars is better than our common seltzer. Half a jar is sufficient for a bowl of Imperial. The quantities given here are calculated for six to eight persons. If you have champagne in half-bottles, half the quantities indicated may be used—say for a select potatory circle of four—the best way of squaring the circle I know.

ICED MIXED ARRACK AND RUM PUNCH.—Take a pound of sugar, and moisten it in a bowl with four ounces of clear lemon juice. Add boiling water just sufficient to reduce the sugar to syrup. Let it cool; when quite cold, add a few drops of essence of lemon on a lump of sugar, and the juice of six or eight fine oranges. Put in a pound of ice in small pieces, and pour in a gill each of old Jamaica rum and arrack. The spirit will rapidly melt the ice, which will turn the mass into a freezing mixture. Add a bottle of champagne—Saumur will do. Half of a pint bottle of Dublin stout will be found a great improvement. The late Thomas Littleton Holt, who was a dear friend of mine and a great punchmaker, never omitted the stout from his brews in this line.

STRAWBERRY PUNCH.—This delightful beverage is made with STRAWBERRY EXTRACT or RUM for chief ingredient. As strawberry rum, properly bottled, will keep a full twelvemonth in a good cellar or other suitable place, sufficient may be prepared of it in the season to last till next summer. The proportion is one pound of strawberries to every pint of spirit. Crush the fresh gathered strawberries—the small wild ones are the most fragrant—in a capacious stone or earthen crock, and transfer the mash in equal portions to large stone or glass jars, with tight-closing stoppers or lids, and add to the contents of each jar an equal quantity of one pint to every pound of strawberries of a mixture of two-thirds of the finest old Jamaica rum and one-sixth pint each of the best arrack and old Cognac. Close the jars, and let them stand three days in a cool place, opening them from time to time to give them a stir with a stout glass rod. Then pour off the liquid from each jar gradually into another large crock, through a rather coarse hair sieve, to which transfer finally also the residuary pulp from the jar, working it through. Let the last portion of liquid still remaining in the dregs drain off into the crock, through a clean linen cloth that has been washed in boiling water and dried again.

Bottle the Strawberry Rum or Extract in Imperial quart bottles, cork and seal these and lay them down horizontally in a dry cool cellar or other suitable place.

The dregs will yield a very good punch, with about half a pint of the mixed spirit added, and the proper proportion of boiling water poured over, with sugar and lemon juice to taste.

To make Strawberry Punch, moisten a pound and a half of sugar in a bowl with five to six ounces of clear fresh lemon juice, add two drops each of lemon and orange essence, and pour in one of your imperial quarts of Strawberry Rum—stir the mixture, and add two quarts of boiling water. Cover the bowl, and let it stand till the evening, when you will find it a truly delicious liquor. Bottled, it will keep four or five days; the bottles should always be laid horizontally.

There are two high ecclesiastic-dignitary drinks, yclept severally CARDINAL and BISHOP. They are both made chiefly with extracts.

To make CARDINAL EXTRACT, take two ounces and a half of coarsely pounded cinnamon, half an ounce of vanilla cut into small pieces, and the yellow rind of four or five oranges with the peel of one lemon ; put these ingredients into a suitable glass jar with proper stopper, and pour over them three half pints of the best arrack and a wineglassful each of old Cognac and Jamaica rum. Close the jar and let the ingredients digest three days in a warm place, with repeated shaking. Then filter the contents through Swedish filtering paper, bottle and cork and keep for use. Add one ounce of the extract to a bottle of fine Rhine wine, and sweeten to taste. About a quarter of a pound of sugar will do.

For BISHOP EXTRACT take the rind of twelve fresh green oranges, shaved off as thin as practicable, and let them digest in the same way as stated in the Cardinal recipe, in a pint of rectified spirit of wine in lieu of arrack, and add one ounce of the extract to a bottle of fine Bordeaux or Burgundy.

There are two principal varieties of PUNCH EXTRACT —for Arrack Punch and for Rum Punch.

For ARRACK PUNCH EXTRACT.—Boil one pound and a half of sugar with three quarters of a pint of water, add eight ounces of fresh clear lemon juice to the

solution, with three drops each of essence of lemon and
orange, and let it get cold. Then add a bottle of the
finest arrack with a gill of old Jamaica rum. For
Punch, one quart of the extract is used to two parts
of boiling water.

The RUM PUNCH EXTRACT is made in exactly the
same way, only substituting a bottle of the best old
Jamaica rum with a gill of arrack, for the bottle of
arrack and the gill of rum.

A very excellent WINE PUNCH.—Put eighteen ounces
of sugar in a suitable enamelled saucepan, pour in six
bottles of Laubenheimer or Niersteiner; and heat to
boiling on a gentle fire. Add a pint of arrack or a
pint of rum, or a mixture in equal proportions of the
two, and leave it a short time longer on the fire, but do
not let it come to the boil again. A few drops of lemon
or orange essence may be added; also two ounces of
fresh clear lemon juice.

Or heat four bottles of Laubenheimer or Niersteiner
or some other light Rhine wine in an enamelled saucepan to boiling, add a quart of tea (made with about three
quarters of an ounce of fine gunpowder), half a pound
of sugar, two ounces of fresh clear lemon juice, and a
few drops of lemon essence. Transfer the mixture to
the bowl, and add a pint of arrack or rum.

HOT WINE—This is made best in a fire-proof earthen
pot with lid. Put in an ounce of fine cinnamon broken

in small pieces, a pound of loaf sugar, and four bottles of fairly good Bordeaux or Burgundy. Put on the lid, and set the pot on the fire. When just boiling, transfer to the bowl, and add a few drops of essence of lemon. In default of a fire-proof earthen pot, a good enamelled stewpan or saucepan will do.

An excellent MIXED WINE PUNCH—Dissolve two pounds of loaf sugar in a quart of cold tea made with an ounce of gunpowder, and two bottles of good Bordeaux wine; flavour it with a few drops of mixed essence of cinnamon, vanilla, and lemon; add two bottles of good Burgundy, two of hock, one of sound sherry, one of old port, and a pint bottle of Madeira; stir. Put two pounds of ice in small pieces in a very capacious bowl or crock, and pour over them a pint and a half of a mixture in equal proportions of old Cognac, rum, and arrack; add the wine, &c., mixture at once, and pour in one or two bottles of Champagne. Add one wineglassful each of green Chartreuse, and of dry Curaçao.

ATHOL BROSE—An ancient mariner, whom I met casually at the Ship Tavern, in Edinburgh, initiated me into the mysteries of this famous tipple. I will give his recipe just as he gave it to me. Pour a pint and a half of boiling water over four ounces of best honey in a bowl, and stir vigorously; add the juice of half a lemon, with the peel thereof finely shaved off. Pour in

a quart of sound old whisky, and ladle out. He told
me, with a wink, that whisky was always best minus
the "ill-flavoured" ingredient of the "Inland Revenue"
department. The experience I have had of Poteen and
other "ungaugered" whiskies makes me much inclined
to indorse the ancient mariner's views upon the
subject.

Here I must stop. The "Laws of Space" are as
inexorable as the Laws of the Medes.

THE END.

—TAG—

which may serve equally for Preface,

TO

BYRON WEBBER.

Here is the Book. I am sadly afraid you will not find it the Thusnelda Irma production you not unlikely expected to see. A good-natured lady acquaintance, who has read over some of the proofs, tells me, with the cruel candour of benevolent friendship, that she finds little philosophy in the book, and less kitchen. I daresay she is right; but I know there is one thing that might be allowed to count for something—to wit, earnest, honest work.

THE NEW NOVELS AT EVERY LIBRARY.

THE SACRED NUGGET. By B. L. FARJEON, Author of "Great Porter Square : A Mystery," &c. 3 vols. 31s. 6d.

MORNING GREY. By the Author of "Ade." 3 vols. 31s. 6d.

THE FLOWER OF DOOM. By M. BETHAM-EDWARDS, Author of "Kitty," "Pearla," &c. 1 vol. 6s.

LIKE LOST SHEEP : A Riverside Story. By ARNOLD GRAY, Author of "The Wild Warringtons," &c. 3 vols. 31s. 6d.

A MAIDEN ALL FORLORN. By the Author of "Phyllis," "Molly Bawn," &c. 3 vols. 31s. 6d.

LIL LORIMER. By THEO GIFT, Author of "A Matter of Fact Girl," &c. 3 vols. 31s. 6d.

SOME STAINED PAGES : A Story of Life. By the Author of "The New Mistress," &c. 3 vols. 31s. 6d.

THE PRETTIEST WOMAN IN WARSAW. By MABEL COLLINS, Author of " In the Flower of Her Youth," &c. Second Edition. 3 vols. 31s. 6d.

NOT EVERY DAY : A Love Octave. By CONSTANCE MACEWEN, Author of " Miss Beauchamp." 2 vols. 21s.

JOHN FORD. By FRANK BARRETT, Author of "Honest Davie," &c. 2 vols. 12s.

12, YORK STREET, COVENT GARDEN, LONDON.

Lightning Source UK Ltd.
Milton Keynes UK
UKOW04f0807280915

259388UK00001B/112/P